TIDY UP OR SIMPLIFY

Tidy Up or SIMPLIFY

{ THE DIFFERENCE IS WHAT WILL CHANGE YOUR LIFE }

BRITA LONG

LIONCREST
PUBLISHING

TIDY UP OR SIMPLIFY

The Difference Is What Will Change Your Life

ISBN   978-1-5445-1483-3 *Hardcover*

978-1-5445-1482-6 *Paperback*

978-1-5445-1481-9 *Ebook*

For my mother, Beatrice Long, who taught me how to live an authentically simple and good life, without focusing on the stuff. And to all who read this book and have the courage to go against the grain and create a life that fits them.

CONTENTS

INTRODUCTION 9

1. I HAVE DONE IT 17

2. DO YOU HAVE TOO MUCH STUFF? 23

3. WHAT THE EXTRA STUFF COSTS US AND HOW IT HARMS OUR BRAINS 37

4. WHY IS IT SO HARD TO GET RID OF OUR STUFF? 69

5. WHY WE BUY SO MUCH STUFF 87

6. WHAT THE HELL DO YOU WANT? 107

7. THE ACTUAL PURGING, ONCE AND FOR ALL 127

8. MOVING FORWARD 153

9. THE FALLOUT 169

10. FREEDOM, THE REAL PRIZE 181

CONCLUSION 191

ACKNOWLEDGMENTS 195

ABOUT THE AUTHOR 199

INTRODUCTION

When is enough, enough? You thought you were going to be happy when you bought that handbag. You just knew you were going to feel secure when you owned "enough" clothes or had $X in the bank. That feeling of not being good enough was going to go away when you finally purchased that new high-end luxury car. You were really, *finally*, going to be happy and secure when you moved into that big house, with the stone countertops and custom closets. You imagined you were going to be happy when you could afford that trip to Europe. If you just worked hard enough to make that extra whatever per year so that you could buy whatever—then, *then* you would be happy and content. You would have gotten *there*. You would have *made* it. You also would have shown the world that you amounted to someone; you were smart enough, good enough, pretty enough, popular enough, and worth enough.

Instead, year after year passes. We pursue income increase after income increase. We buy handbag after handbag, car after car, book after book, trip after trip, and house after house.

After everything is said and done, what horrible discovery do we make?

We realize that after the initial, far too short, high of possessing *the thing*, we just went back to being us. We return to feeling like the same person we were before we got *the thing*. That isn't a comfortable feeling, and we don't like it. So, what do we do? We almost immediately trick ourselves into moving onto the next *thing*. *That* will be the thing. We do this day after day, year after year, and most of us do it until we die.

For some of us, it is small, relatively inexpensive stuff such as books, kitchen gadgets, or clothing. In some cases, the less one has to pay for the item, the easier it is to justify having it. On the other end of the scale are people who collect real estate, companies, sports teams, or people in the form of employees or groupies/followers. Regardless of the price of the thing one is seeking, the thought process is the same and I would contend the feelings are the same. Whether you continually think the next car, home, or pair of shoes is going to make the difference in your life, the feelings of never having enough are all the same. The motivations are the same. We are all searching to feel accepted, valued, and, dare I say it, loved. We have been taught, and it is reinforced 10,000 times a day, that in order to get that feeling, in order to be *successful*, we need to own or possess X. And that X changes depending on what is being sold to us on that particular day. We generally know it's bullshit, but we keep buying into it time after time without any real regard to the consequences.

Maybe you don't have an issue with the volume of possessions you have, but you have things that don't fit you. Literally and figuratively. You have things that just aren't you. And you continue to buy things that aren't really you. When you have possessions that aren't you or that you don't even really like, you know you shouldn't have them in your life.

Deep down in the recesses of your heart, you know having too much stuff isn't good for you, regardless of what those items are. You know keeping items you don't even really like or use isn't good. Maybe you haven't really thought about the ways the cycle of having too much stuff has really hurt your life, but you know things could be simpler. You may have shame about how much stuff you really have, that you can't keep that closet or room organized, or you have financial stress yet have a ton of crap. You know when you wear that outfit that isn't you, it makes you uncomfortable. You know every time you sit in that chair, regardless of how pretty it might be, it isn't even comfortable. Maybe you are highly educated and smart, yet you can't seem to get control of this one area of your life. At the very least, you know that continually buying stuff shouldn't be a pastime or hobby. You know having fifty cookie cutters is a bit much— right? You know if you died suddenly, someone else would be left with a huge mess to clean up.

The issue isn't *having* things. The issue is *being overly attached* to things, and having your self-worth attached to things—especially things that aren't serving you.

If something isn't right with your life, things aren't working the way you want them to work, or you are not happy and you aren't sure what the problem is, I would suggest starting with simplifying your life and specifically simplifying your stuff. Why? Because deep down, we all yearn for simplicity. We yearn to have our world and our stuff fit us. We want our things to reflect who we are, what we love, and what we value—and have them work for us. What could be simpler than that?

Our gut, instinct, soul, or whatever else you want to call it, knows that we do better with simple. We are happier with simple. We are less depressed, anxious, and taxed with simple. You may not understand right now why you were drawn to this book, but my guess is that deep down you too are yearning for a simpler way of living.

Specifically, in this culture we are constantly told we need the next shiny ball that will make us happy when we possess it. We will only be a good person, a good wife, a good father, successful, sexy, or happy when we own it. Unfortunately, we believe the message. I continued chasing the shiny ball for decades, until I was so unhappy and frustrated that I knew something had to change—and not by a little bit.

Only when I finally accepted that the problem didn't have anything to do with organizing the stuff or the stuff itself, but me—and only me—did things begin to change in my life. Only then did I break free from wanting anything that didn't serve me or wasn't truly me.

Who the hell am I to be teaching you about simplification and what you *should* or *shouldn't* own? I am an attorney, a mother, a businesswoman, an author, a retired amateur trapeze artist, a speaker, and a mentor. I have wing-walked over the Salish Sea and have a ton of moxie and courage. I have practiced law for more than two decades and have seen behind the curtain into countless people's lives and their relationships with stuff. None of that is why you should listen to me. You should listen to me because I have been in the same place you are, more than once, and I found the way out. It isn't the easy way or the fast way, but it is the way I found to get to the root of the stuff issue. It is the way to rid yourself, once and for all, of any desire to have anything in your life that doesn't serve you. To get rid of any desire for excess. To only have the best in your life and to create a life that fits you.

Other methods only dealt with getting rid of stuff—not why you had it in the first place. My method is starting with inner work and one's ego before we begin to sort through any stuff.

If you are reading this hoping for a quick, easy, ten-step process to finally and permanently fix your stuff problem, then this is NOT the book for you. Just like everything else in life, there is no simple, quick, and easy fix to a complex problem. And you have most likely already tried some of the other quick and easy solutions to fixing your stuff problem and found that after a short time they didn't work. Why? Because...it was never really about the stuff.

My method to simplify requires you to do some difficult inner examination before you even consider getting rid of your stuff. We are tearing down a weak foundation and completely rebuilding it with healthy beliefs. I need to warn you that this can be difficult work and you may get impatient with the process. When you start thinking, "Man, I wish she would just get to the steps on how to get rid of crap," that is probably just your ego resisting the work that really needs to be done.

So, you can just tidy up, or you can do the work and completely simplify your life. However, the only way to free yourself from an unhealthy attachment to stuff is to do the hard work.

My hope is to save you from the pain that I had to go through, in order to get to the point of only having what serves you in your life. This book suggests a method of simplifying your life that, after some hard work, will make it easy for you to create a life that works for you.

My method is NOT about me, or anyone else, telling you how many items of property you should own—how many shirts, books, kitchen items, or anything else you should own or how to organize or fold clothing. Folding clothing nicely is lovely, but I would argue it has nothing to do with simplifying your life. Further, it is not sustainable.

Many people have tried to simplify in the past; maybe you have as well. Just like me, they want a simpler life. They want to get rid of their excess stuff. So, they buy a book, look at a video, hire an organizer, get excited, and immediately start to get rid of stuff. It is a lot of hard work, but they feel wonderful with a less cluttered home. Then, within a few months, new things begin to appear in their home. Just little things at first. The spare room starts to have things on the bed—temporarily. Then, within a year, they are back to having to clear off the kitchen table in order to have a meal or parking on the driveway as they can't park in the garage again.

My method is about really getting to the root of the issue, not just continuing to cut back leaves only to have them grow back. There are no miracle cures, just honest hard work. In my method, we address the emotional issue first, and then everything falls in line. It is easy to get rid of what doesn't serve you, once you have addressed your emotions around stuff. But until you address the emotions, you will always be in the cycle of having too much stuff.

So please trust the process and be patient.

Is reading this book going to change your life? Absolutely not. Will reading this book and taking the time to do the hard work and self-examination change your life? It certainly has the power to, but not instantly and only if you are honest with yourself, feel the feelings, and do the work.

So, are you ready to get real, do the hard work, and reap the rewards? If the answer is yes, keep reading.

CHAPTER 1

I HAVE DONE IT

Why should you listen to me? Because I have done it. I have had the same challenges you have had, the same frustrations, and the same feelings. I am a woman who has banged her head against a wall umpteen dozen times trying desperately to get "it," only to find that I didn't feel any differently once I got "it." I am a woman who continually thought that the next thing would make me happy, over and over again. The next thing, book, car, trip, diamond, French mirror, house, and business would finally give me the feeling of being successful and get me accepted into an invisible club. I am someone who blew opportunity after opportunity over chasing the stuff—the next shiny ball. I thought that ball would make me feel accepted, successful, respected, and worthy of being loved. This cycle left me demoralized, frustrated, and feeling shame.

Even when I began to wake up about what buying and having excess stuff was doing to my life and how it was hurting me, I still struggled with it until I had what can only be described as a "simplicity breakdown." I finally began to change my entire view of the stuff and how I felt about it. I finally was so unhappy and filled with so much stress and anxiety that I knew I couldn't go on living the way I had been living. Something had to change. Something big had to change.

So, I bought and read the books, read the blogs, and watched the TED Talks on simplification. I knew I wanted and needed a simpler life but wasn't sure how to get it or even what it would look like. Much of the advice on simplifying life actually made things worse. I wanted simple, not extreme.

I wanted a simpler life, a really simple life, but I didn't want to live in a tiny house. I liked electricity, running water, and indoor plumbing. I certainly didn't want to have to gather my own food from trees (yes, that was one simplification video I saw). I was an attorney. I needed more clothing than would fit in one carry-on suitcase. I also didn't need to be taught how to fold my clothing. I bristled at someone who had never met me telling me how many shirts I should own or anything else. Huh? Who the hell are you to tell me how many of X is acceptable for me to own?

I wanted my life to be simple but still fit me. I liked nice things. I wanted to keep some of my nice things. I wanted a big life, a superb life, just not all of the stuff. I wanted the life that fit me, not someone else's version of my life or someone else's rules about what I should have, or not. Much of the advice I heard or read might have fit the person prescribing it, but it wasn't necessarily meant to fit their audience, and it most certainly didn't fit the life I wanted.

And to top it all off, none of it worked—for very long, that is. Yeah, I would watch an episode of *Hoarders*, read a new book, throw out a bunch of stuff, and feel better—but nothing in my life changed. I didn't have a simpler life. On top of that, most of the time, within a year or so, I would just go and get more or different stuff. I wanted a simple life but was still very attached to impressing others with my beautiful stuff.

It wasn't until I got so tired of my life, so frustrated that I was well past the point of screaming, that I gave up. I just gave up. What I had been doing clearly wasn't working in life. I was hard-working, smart, and ambitious, and what I was doing wasn't working. I was going to get the simpler life I wanted, the life that fit me, no matter what it meant. Even if it meant giving up many of my nice things, including my beautiful home. Only when I was ready to give up my attachment, completely, to anything that wasn't serving me did things begin to change.

I am a woman who figured out, after trying everything else, how to live a simple and superb life that has actually stuck.

Instinctively, I knew that I had to start with the stuff. I don't know why I knew, but I knew that this journey had to begin with the stuff. I began to feel compelled to get rid of stuff. And when I say compelled, that is what I mean. I started getting rid of things left and right. I just wanted the stuff gone and out of my life.

This process meant that I had to be honest with myself, a level of honesty that I had never come close to before. I had to admit things I never wanted to admit. I had to see things about myself I didn't want to see. I had to admit to all of the money I had wasted buying stuff in order to impress other people or to make myself feel "successful." I had to admit that I had gone overboard buying gifts, many of which I couldn't afford, to get people to appreciate me. I had to admit that even though I had spent a lot of time, money, and effort to make that room or house beautiful, it wasn't "me." It didn't "fit" me. I had to admit that I had made so many purchases trying to run away from the poor little trailer-trash girl I thought I really was, even though I have never lived in a trailer.

My honesty with myself freed me from the stuff. And if you are truly honest with yourself, you can be free as well. This does not include shaming yourself. Growth is not possible with shame.

You can be free from having your self-worth attached to stuff. Free from worrying about what other people think about what you have or don't have. Free from ever wanting anything that isn't benefitting you, that you don't really want, or isn't really "you."

So, if anything in my story resonates with you, then I would urge you to keep reading. If I was able to free myself from my overconsumption, overspending, and attachment to stuff, so can you. I will show you how.

{ CHAPTER 2 }

DO YOU HAVE TOO MUCH STUFF?

"I had plans for that rock!"

—A HOARDER, FROM THE TV SHOW *HOARDERS*

"One bar of soap every four weeks; thirteen bars of soap per year; fifty-eight bars of soap will last almost four and a half years. I have four-and-a-half years' worth of soap in my linen closet. Is that enough? Well, yes, but the price will only increase, they aren't going to go bad, and I have room to store them, so maybe I'll buy just one or two more packs (with sixteen bars per pack) the next time I go to Costco."

—ME, IN MY BRAIN, JUSTIFYING WHY
I BOUGHT YET MORE SOAP

The first quote, above, is from a hoarder. On the show, she would not get rid of anything and her sister, in frustration, picked up a rock the hoarder had been keeping and threw it across the yard. Her response? "I had plans for that rock!"

One of the thoughts that kept coming up for me when I would watch the show *Hoarders* was how absolutely powerful denial could be for people. Parents, who did really love their children, were literally days away from having their children removed from their care due to the state of their home, and they would still say, "It isn't that bad." Other people were days away from losing their home, due to having so much stuff inside and outside of the home. They would still fight tooth and nail to keep the stuff, even though it was crap and destroying their and their children's lives. That is how powerful denial is.

It is easy to look at other people, who clearly have a problem with stuff, with a combination of shock, disgust, and relief. Relief in that at least you "aren't *that* bad." We judge others as a way of separating ourselves from them—able to feel better about ourselves because at least we are not as bad off as they are.

If you are going to be completely honest with yourself though, maybe you are. No, you don't have spoiled food sitting in your house and you can walk throughout your house easily. But you still have that "collection" of hundreds of magazines that you are never going to read. You have that stash of fabric that even if you sewed eight hours a day, every day for the rest of your life, you wouldn't use all of it. You have jewelry piece after jewelry piece that you don't wear, or those tools you are keeping because you *may* use them someday. You still have boxes you haven't even unpacked from moving two years ago. And for those who love to read, do I need to mention the books?

When I write about excess goods, I am including the items that aren't really you. It isn't just about how many things you have, but whether or not you even really like those things.

For me, the things I loved were household goods. The real problem started after I graduated law school and got a job at Williams Sonoma while waiting for my bar exam results. I had always loved the store, and I cooked and baked. We got a 40 percent discount on anything in the store, or from Pottery Barn. I was using twenty-plus-year-old thin towels, mismatched twenty-year-old cheap sheets, and everything in my kitchen I had gotten at yard sales and I didn't feel proud to use. The products at Williams Sonoma were better than anything I had ever seen, much less used. They were beautiful and of high quality, and I felt good just being in the store—and I would have them for life. *This* was an investment. I also would never get another chance like this—40 percent off? Are you kidding me? Of course I am buying the stuff, and as much as I can get my hands on.

I also wanted to provide my son with a nice home and nice

things so he could be proud and not embarrassed when friends came over, although he had never been embarrassed to have friends over previously. Our home had always been clean, tidy, and nice. However, I wanted him to experience having nicer things, even though he could have cared less about the thread count of the sheets he was sleeping in.

I also wanted to feel normal and have what other people had. Actually, I wanted more than normal. No one else I knew had a full set of All-Clad cookware. My point is that some of my reasons for wanting to buy things at Williams Sonoma did serve me. They certainly made rational sense, to a point. However, many others were totally tied into my ego.

From the first day I qualified for my discount, I went nuts. Absolutely nuts. I would walk out of the store with four huge bags nearly every shift. I had the largest set of cookware you could get and still had additional pieces. Even though I had never had more than two people over for dinner, I had a set of dinnerware for twelve. I continue to use that set every day mind you, but still. I had two different kinds of electric juicers, plus two manual ones. Don't get me started on how many cookbooks I had. At one point I had three, yes three, butter curlers. One was modern, for those hip dinner parties; one was fancy, for the queen; and one was for everyday use. How many times do you think I used any of the butter curlers? Not once.

My little apartment looked like a combination of Pottery Barn and Williams Sonoma. Even though I put every purchase I made on a credit card, I still felt great. I had a home I was proud of. I had stuff people commented on. People wanted to cook in my kitchen because I had the cool stuff. I felt wonderful, for a short time.

When I look back at it now though, probably well over half, if not more, of the stuff I bought was ridiculous, I didn't use, and I don't have today. However, this hit of juice really started my buying frenzies.

Within months of starting at Williams Sonoma, I got my first job as an attorney. I had a tiny bit of disposable income for the first time in my life. After feeling deprived for so many years, or so I told myself, I kept on buying—even though my home already looked like a store. Now I also "had" to look the part of a professional. Yes, I did need new items of clothing, but no, I didn't need as many as I got.

I never wanted to want for anything in my home. So, I started to stock up at Costco. Toiletries, soaps, toilet paper, cleaning supplies, and other consumables were a hot ticket for me. Yes, as referenced at the beginning of this chapter, at one point I figured out I had enough soap for over four years. And I still felt like one more pack would make me feel better, more secure.

My type of collecting differed, along with the severity of the hoarding, but my thought process really wasn't that different from the lady who "had plans for that rock." Whether it was a rock or a nice handbag, "one more" was going to make me feel better. The category of stuff is irrelevant.

I have a friend whose thing was old magazines and fabric. I have another dear friend, Karen, who quilts. She needs fabric to quilt, *and* she has enough fabric, right now, that if she quilted fourteen hours a day, every single day until she was 120 years old, she would still not use all of the fabric she has currently. Yet, she still buys more.

I have another friend, Amanda, who went to art school. She took out extra student loans to buy very expensive Dutch oil paint. Over fifteen years later, and after many moves, she still has many cans of that paint unopened.

The first step in examining your relationship with stuff is to get real. Real with yourself. Don't get me wrong, we are smart. We can rationalize keeping anything. Just know that rationalizing is lying to yourself, and you are only hurting yourself by doing so.

So, what is your "thing"? What do you have that you know is excessive? If you even have one piece of clothing that you don't feel great about wearing, much less doesn't actually fit you, then you have excess stuff. If you are keeping even one book for the "someday" that you might read that book, it is excess.

If you are ready to be honest with yourself, then keep reading. Move forward *without* judgment or shame. There are reasons you have too much stuff. We will get to those reasons. None of them include the fact that you are a bad person, stupid, fucked up, or any other quality that deserves shame. Be kind to yourself, please.

Do you have too much stuff?

If your most honest and immediate answer is not a solid "no," then the answer is really yes. If there is even a hint of defensiveness or rationalization, or you can't keep a totally straight face, then the answer is yes. If your first thought was "No, and here is why," then it is really a yes. Here are some more indications that yes, you have too much stuff:

- Anyone has ever suggested, in any way, that perhaps you have a lot of stuff.
- You have clothing that doesn't fit you and you are not comfortable wearing, or you have thirty cups in the cupboard but only use the same ten over and over again.
- You buy things because they are pretty or cool but find that you don't use them.
- You have ever found yourself short on money, yet you have a home full of stuff or relatively expensive items.

- You have any trouble getting rid of stuff—anything.
- You are spending money to store stuff, for more than just a temporary situation.
- You are spending any time or money to care for items you don't use on a regular basis.
- You have ever felt the need to explain, even to yourself, why you have X, Y, or Z.
- You couldn't use all of X in one to two years or even your damn lifetime.
- Stuff has caused strife in a relationship.
- Someone else has suggested you read this book.
- You justify keeping stuff by thinking that you can solve the problem by just organizing it properly.
- You are interested in reading this book.

If you identify with any of the statements above, then yes, you probably have too much stuff.

The answer is generally *always* going to be "Yes, I have too much stuff." Because if it were a true no, neither you nor anyone else would ever question it. The "no" answers are self-evident. If you are a baker and have three baking pans, no one would ever question if that is too much.

The property that we need, is useful to us, and feels like an extension of ourselves is all fairly self-evident. If it isn't self-evident, then at the least keep an open mind about whether it is too much.

Are you not ready to admit there is an issue, but still willing to keep reading? That's okay, friend—this is a process. Thank you for your willingness to stay with it. As we go forward, please remember that you are probably going to be tempted to rationalize keeping stuff. Denial is denial, and it can be just as strong as for the woman who is about to lose her kids to CPS yet wants to keep the stuff. Just be aware of when you start to get defensive or feel the need to protect that thing—again, even just to yourself. We get defensive because the truth hurts, and that is something you may want to pay attention to.

Also remember: I am not going to suggest you get rid of anything that is serving you or that you love. My method isn't about living with no personal property, living in a tiny house, or any other extremes. This is only about examining your property and keeping what really serves you and fits you.

Because if it isn't really serving you, then it is *hurting* you.

Do you really want a simpler life?

What? What kind of stupid question is that? Bear with me, friend. There are a lot of people who say they want something, actually think they want something, but really don't. Maybe something hidden deep inside of them, even subconsciously, is holding them back or self-sabotaging them.

I know this sounds like woo-woo crap, but it isn't. There are a lot of reasons you have a more complicated life or more stuff than works well in your life. Some of this I will address in chapters 3 and 4. If you are not at least partially open to that possibility, there will always be an invisible wall keeping you from going where you say you want to go.

People only get what they think they are worthy of receiving. It took me a long time to understand and accept this, but it is true. They also generally only change something negative when the pain to change is less than the current pain itself. Yes, there are those proactive people who are on the lookout for self-improvement before there is a major problem, but the rest of us generally only put down the donut when we can't fit into our clothes or we feel a chest pain.

This book is not a motivational, feel-good-for-a-few-hours type of book. This is serious and hard work that you are going to be doing—if you choose to do so. You have to feel that you are *worthy* of a simpler, better way of life—a life that fits who you are on the inside. And you are going to have to be willing to go through a bit of discomfort in order to get there.

Also recognize that you, along with everyone else, get something out of your dysfunction, complex life, or chaos. What you are getting may not be self-evident, but it is always there. What you are *getting* generally isn't something positive, either. We do a lot to stay with what we know, what is comfortable to us—even if it is hurting us. Probably the best example of this is people staying in a job that makes them miserable but justifying it because it pays the bills. They stay in that job year after year, because it is more comfortable to stay than look for another job or take a risk with a new job.

So, at some level, you are actively choosing the chaos, dysfunction, and pain because you are getting something out of it. You would rather stay in the comfort zone you know. We all have invisible, unconscious barriers that are meant to protect us. They may have been helpful at one time in our lives, but they are no longer helping us. Now they are hurting us. Unless we do the work to be able to see where these barriers are in our subconscious, we will forever be blocked by the barriers *every single time*.

The best way in which I can describe this is through an example.

I tend to make my life far more difficult and chaotic than it needs to be. At one point in my life, I needed to do really hard things. I was a very young teenage mom who worked her way through college and law school. I had a law degree by age twenty-six and a law license six months later. My working like I was on fire propelled me to do amazing things...until it began to get in my way.

Buy a normal house? Not Brita. No, I buy an old home that needs to be taken down to the studs and fully renovated, not once but twice. Just get a rescue dog. Nope. I only want the dogs with behavior problems, please. Marry a nice guy? No, thank you. I will marry the man who loves me but is an alcoholic and can be emotionally abusive, thank you. Take my time to move across the country? Nope, I will sell my home, buy another one, close down a law practice, and move—all within two months. I could provide example after example of how I used to make my life far harder and more complex than it needed to be. I would actually brag that "I don't do easy" like it was a badge of honor. I was used to hard. I was comfortable with hard. Easy was for lazy people. Easy was for people who couldn't handle difficult.

In reality, I was making my life far more difficult than it needed to be. That was the case until I was able to recognize what I was doing, examine why, and change the behavior and pattern. My life didn't need to be hard. I wasn't lazy if I didn't make things as hard as humanly possible. I didn't need to hand cut a log when a power saw was available. I could begin to make choices that would produce a simpler, easier life. I didn't need to prove anything to myself or prove that I was a hard worker by making things more difficult than they needed to be.

This work takes time, self-reflection, and exercises that some would consider to be woo-woo but are actually just feeling feelings deep within you. Without doing this work, you will simply purge some crap, feel great for a few days, and then start back up again. Nothing will change.

My method of simplifying has helped me and others free ourselves from having any desire to have excess stuff, and we've simplified life as a result. But it will only help those who are willing to "go there" and be uncomfortable for a little bit.

A note on the exercises at the end of each chapter:

Do them. Reading this book will give you a bit of knowledge. Knowledge doesn't change behavior, and behavior is what is going to either keep you in the same place or change your life. Doing the exercises is the only way in which you will even have a shot at diving deeper, to where change can take place. You may have to do them a few times, which is completely fine. But if you don't do them, your behavior is not going to change. It just won't.

Please have a journal dedicated just to this work on simplification. Writing out the question and the answer does help our brain and heart absorb the work more fully, so please take the time to do this.

THE WORK

1. Do you have extra stuff?
2. Do you really want a simpler life?
3. If you do want a simpler life, why?
4. Are you willing to do the work necessary to get that simpler life?
5. Why now?
6. What are some ways in which you self-sabotage?
7. If you feel any hesitation or resistance to moving forward, please just sit with that feeling for a few moments, acknowledge it, and ask yourself why you are feeling the resistance.

CHAPTER 3

WHAT THE EXTRA STUFF COSTS US AND HOW IT HARMS OUR BRAINS

"Many wealthy people are little more than janitors of their possessions."

—FRANK LLOYD WRIGHT

"When the billionaire was asked how much was 'enough,' he replied, 'Just a little bit more.'"

—UNKNOWN

Remember when I wrote that this work could be uncomfortable? Well, here we go, friend. It might be tempting to skip over this chapter, or rush through it, but please don't cheat yourself by not reading this chapter in full and feeling the feelings that come up when you read it. Feeling those feelings and sitting with them is where the magic happens. We can't change something that we don't acknowledge AND feel. Remember the goal is not just to get rid of some crap—it is to change your relationship with stuff.

We all recognize (for the most part) that too much of anything, even a good thing, is bad for us. Too much play becomes boring. Even spending too much time with people we love can be too much. My aunt used to say that company was like fish. It is great for three days and then it starts to stink. Too much exercise hurts our muscles and joints. A little bit of fire keeps us warm and cooks our food. Too much fire causes destruction.

Yet, many of us don't recognize that too much stuff really does hurt us, whether we can financially afford the stuff or not. The price that we pay for having excess stuff in our lives is far more than money. In addition to the financial aspect, there are far more subtle impacts to our lives that come from having excess stuff.

MONEY

We spend a lot of money to feed our ego by buying more stuff. It is our ego who is continually telling us that we aren't thin enough or wealthy enough, that we need to buy that new item in order to be or look "successful," or that what we have isn't "enough." When our ego, or self-esteem, is tied to what we own, we are going to be spending a lot of money and it will never be enough.

Take it from someone who knows. If your ego is tied to your stuff, you will always have financial stress (or at the very least waste a whole lot of money) until you get a handle on your ego. And having financial stress is miserable.

Two of the times that I have experienced extreme financial stress have been due to my *need* to not only own a home but also fully renovate that home to a luxury level—and to do so as quickly as possible. In the second home, that meant renovating 1,900 square feet in less than six months. It turned out that the home was in far worse shape than I first knew, and the renovation ended up costing me every penny I had ever made and still put me in debt. When you have just lost everything, are still in debt, and are under huge financial stress for a house—a damn house—you begin to conduct some serious introspection. This is the point when I knew that I had to drastically alter the way I thought and felt about the stuff. This was my rock bottom, my simplicity breakdown.

My emotional and mental health had to be more important than owning a large home with marble countertops.

If you have ever faced financial stress as an adult, you are not alone. You are also not stupid, although it can feel that way. Some fairly intelligent people have been in the same boat, including presidents Thomas Jefferson, Abraham Lincoln, and John Adams.

Regardless of your financial status, a portion of the root cause of financial stress for the vast majority of people is spending more on stuff, or our lifestyle, than is within our means. Few of us truly have the funds to just waste on items that we don't need and don't bring us joy for more than a few minutes. And frankly, it doesn't matter how much money you have. We hear story after story of multimillionaire entertainers, lottery winners, and others going broke because they bought too much stuff. Yes, the stuff they bought was probably a lot more expensive than what you buy, but the behavior and thought pattern is the same. They just bought Ferraris, houses, and $2,000 shoes, when you are buying less expensive items.

We've all known people who have a closet bursting with clothes yet scrimp on other life necessities such as healthy food or medicine, or the person who has nearly every video game ever made and yet doesn't have $500 in savings. Pick any other example you want—the behavior is the same.

Again, it isn't just the people whose buying is causing financial hardship to them or in other ways limiting their lifestyle. Even the people who "can afford" to have extra stuff are financially impacted by buying and caring for stuff they don't need or really want.

To demonstrate just what a financial impact too much stuff has, I want you to do a short but incredibly powerful thing. You are not going to want to do it. You may come up with 101 reasons why you don't have the time, this is stupid, you don't do exercises in books, etc. That resistance you are feeling is just your brain and ego trying to protect yourself from some ugly damn truth and pain. It is going to be uncomfortable. You may want to vomit. Do it anyway. The only way to get to the other side is to go through this crap.

I have done this exercise with wealthy individuals who have more money than most of us can imagine, and I have also done the exercise with people who are really struggling. It is powerful regardless of your financial situation.

I want you to pick one category of items: shoes, clothing, makeup, tools, books, whatever it is that you have too much of. Then, go through every single item in that category and separate the items that you really don't use or love. BE HONEST. If you say you truly love all 1,001 antique rugs, I am calling bullshit. You love the idea of having them all, but no, you don't love them all equally. If the house were on fire and you only had time to grab two or three, which would they be? Just saying you love them all is being lazy and not wanting to do the hard work.

Separate the books that you are not going to read in the future. The clothing you haven't worn in a year. The shoes that hurt your feet so badly you are in tears after half an hour of wearing them. Household furnishings that aren't even "you." The tools that, yes, you could use in the future, but haven't in the last year or so.

This is without judgment, without "yeah, buts." I am NOT asking you to get rid of those items. I really am not. If you start getting resistance with an item or start getting defensive or thinking the "yeah, buts," put it in the "maybe I don't love it" pile. We are NOT purging anything...yet. At the end of this exercise, you can put everything back where you got it.

The "yeah, buts" are anything similar to: yeah, but I paid a lot of money for that; it is worth a lot of money; someone else in my family could use it in the future; I could use it in the future; I need that so people know I am a professional; it isn't hurting me to keep it; I need that to show people I am successful, and people don't want to do business with people who are not successful; or, but I got a great deal on that. And the list goes on and on.

Now that you have your "don't love" pile, I want you to—as accurately as possible—calculate what you spent on the pile. Ugh, right? I know you don't want to. It is going to hurt. You are an adult, this is important, and the exercise is important in order to overcome your resistance.

Please don't judge yourself at this stage; just make a mental note of how it feels, and journal about it.

So, what did you, or someone else, spend on your pile? If I offered to give you that amount in cash in exchange for your pile, would you take it?

What we spend on our stuff, even if it is just little by little, twenty-five dollars at a time, adds up. That is fine if we really use or love the stuff. The problem is we don't. We are just throwing money away. That money could be used for things you really want in your life, such as more in savings, retirement, amazing trips, spending time with family, or giving to others and making a real impact in the world.

I want you to notice your feelings after this exercise. Again, I want you to watch the self-judgment and self-talk. This isn't about berating yourself and beating yourself up. There can be no growth when there is self-judgment in the form of shame. All I want is for you to examine your choices and ask yourself if you would rather have the pile of stuff or the money back.

Again, DO NOT take action. I don't want you getting rid of anything yet. I just want you thinking and, more importantly, noticing the feelings that are coming up. If you really want to start moving the needle, start journaling your reactions.

"But I have a shit ton of money," you say. Great, I still want you to do the exercise, and here is why. In my work as an attorney and in my personal life, I have rubbed shoulders with very wealthy people. Incredibly wealthy people. Regardless of your wealth, one needs to be conscious of how one is spending money. Each purchase is a choice. Even if your stuff has never put you in financial stress, it is still wasting your money.

Then there is the issue that your excess buying does actually cause financial harm. Again, we all know of the person who had a shit ton of money and who overspent and lost it. Or committed a crime in order to get money to...buy stuff and lost everything. Or got divorced and lost everything or did drugs and lost it all. You don't have those types of behaviors and that would never happen to you...great. Keep reading anyway.

Regardless of your income or net worth, waste is waste, and it is never a positive thing to have in your life. Someone has traded or is trading their time, energy, and life to earn that money. Do you really want to spend it on stuff that you don't even want or use? Your stuff could be helpful to someone else today instead of sitting around taking up space. Let's say you have $5,000 worth of sports equipment in your garage that is just sitting there, or furniture, jewelry—whatever. Do you have any idea what $5,000 would do for someone else? Do you know what that sports equipment would do for a struggling kid's team? I am not trying to make you feel bad. I am just trying to get you to think about what money is actually being wasted.

> A special note on getting items for free or at an extremely low price. I have had more than one client who prides themselves on getting free clothing at clothing exchanges or buying clothing at thrift stores. I have no problem with buying items at thrift stores or getting items at exchange…as long as you need and love the item and wear it. But that is not what I have found with clients. What I find is that they go nuts and come home with many more items than they would have ever bought normally or will ever wear, and they justify it all by the fact that they paid little or nothing for the stash.

HOUSE

We all need safe shelter. We all want comfortable shelter where we feel good. Our home is our castle. I totally get it. As anyone who knows me will tell you, my home is incredibly important to me. It is my sanctuary. It has always been important to me that it feel and look as good as possible. Even when I was nineteen and a single mom, I went to the dollar store, bought one-dollar flat sheets, and made curtains for my little apartment.

Right now, I am just talking about the actual size of your home. Without judgment, I want you to be honest about what size of home you actually need to live comfortably— not so small that you feel cramped or claustrophobic, but one that you could live in comfortably. Most of us in the US are living in homes that are far larger than we need and many times larger than we really want. What size are you currently living in? What is the monthly cost difference between the two?

Don't freak out. I am NOT suggesting you move or that there is anything wrong with a large home. We are just doing an exercise. This is pretend. Just humor me and do it.

For instance, if you are being totally honest, could you and your family live in a 2,000-square-foot home—comfortably? Most likely yes. And I do mean comfortably, not cramped or uncomfortable in any way. Again, not to the point where you feel claustrophobic. If you are currently living in a 3,500-square-foot home, what is the monthly cost difference between the two? Not just in rent or a mortgage, but if you have a housekeeper, someone mows the lawn, utilities, etc.

For instance, I know a couple who has a beautiful home. It has two spare bedrooms, one of which is a guest suite, as well as a craft room, TV room, formal dining room, family room, and living room. None of those rooms are used more than maybe once every few years. Their home is over 3,500 square feet, yet they really only use probably half of that space. So, my questions are: what is that extra 1,750 square feet, which you don't use, costing you? What is the additional house payment you are making for that space, property taxes, and utilities?

That is it. Just write down a good-faith estimate.

Again, don't freak out. I am not asking that you sell your home and move. Next, I want you to write down how it feels to be living in your space. Is it too small, too big, or just right? If you are in a house that is so small it is causing fights between people, how does that feel? If you are living in a house that is so big people don't interact with one another, it takes staff to keep it up, or there is a lot of wasted space, how does that feel? Just write about your feelings and your house.

TIME

Time is the greatest asset any of us has. You can earn back money; you can never earn back time. Our stuff demands a lot of attention and time, whether it be the time it takes to go to the store and purchase the items or buy online, or the time to clean the stuff, maintain the stuff, or even get rid of the stuff. The more stuff one has, the more time it takes in our lives.

Remember those days when you were a young adult living in a small apartment? It took maybe an hour a week to keep your home clean and tidy. No, you were not responsible for maintenance, but even putting that aside, your living space still didn't demand a lot of your time.

Now, think of the time commitment your stuff takes. How many hours a week does it take to keep your home clean, maintain the yard, clean the pool, take vehicles in for service and keep them clean, organize your stuff, find something you are looking for, and even get rid of your stuff when you want to purge? It adds up to a lot of time.

Even if you are fortunate to be able to afford household help and you aren't the one who is doing the actual cleaning or yard work, it still takes a lot of time, energy, and headache to manage the people who are.

I have a friend, Juanita, who asked me to help her simplify her life. When she first asked me, she and her husband owned nine homes. One of the "homes" was a full working Texas ranch. She and her husband owned their own business and had three kids. She took the primary responsibility for managing the homes. It was really a full-time job, not including managing the ranch. A full-time ranch manager and crew took care of the ranch, other than the main house. They rented out some of the homes on Airbnb. That meant each had to be beautifully decorated, furnished, cleaned several times a week, maintained, and protected.

Even though my friend had lots of help and great professionals working for her, it was all just *soooo* much. The homes were running her life. They were beautiful, and it felt great to drive up to a big beautiful gate with their name on it, but it felt like she was working for her homes, not the other way around.

Yes, that is an extreme example, but the point remains the same. Your stuff takes a lot of your time.

SPACE

To state the obvious, the more stuff you have, the more room you need in order to store the stuff. Again, remember your first apartment, when you had nothing? You could easily live in one bedroom of a small apartment, with roommates. Then we get older, make some money, buy a house, fill up the house, buy another house, fill that up as well, and wake up one day to a massive amount of stuff. No, I am not suggesting that you need to go back to your apartment days of your twenties. What I am saying is that we get into a "chicken and the egg" sort of situation. We need a larger home as we are "busting out at the seams," and when we get the larger space, we instantly fill it and the cycle continues.

Even if you are keeping the home you have and not buying a larger one, my guess is that your stuff is still taking up a lot of literal space in your home. How many people can't park a vehicle in the garage, whose purpose is to store a car, because they have so much other stuff in the garage? I would be willing to bet a sizeable sum that the vast majority of the stuff in those garages isn't being used, isn't really wanted, and is only serving to take up space.

I have looked at plenty of kitchen countertops and thought, "Well, where would one prepare food?" Along with perhaps small appliances that the owners use, such as a toaster, there are plenty of other items that are used maybe once a year. And then there is décor—and a lot of décor. So, you don't have sufficient room to prepare food, in the kitchen, as the counters are filled with items to look good? Does that seem off to you?

Are you having to move things around on your desk or a table just to be able to use it as it was intended, because it is covered with other stuff? Is the stuff that is on the table even supposed to be on the table, or did you just set it down there and never put it away?

And then there is the bathroom. Oh jeez. How many towels does one really need? And let's not forget about all of the old cosmetics, lotions, and other toiletries and hair stuff that we didn't really like, don't use...well it is taking up space. Even if it is just a drawer or two or a few shelves in the linen closet, it is taking up space. I know the pain of trying to find something in a linen closet that has too much stuff in it. No, it isn't a life-altering trauma, but it is a pain in the rear and totally unnecessary.

Then there is the ultimate situation of having so much stuff that your home literally cannot hold it and one has to rent a storage unit, or more than one. There is a reason that the storage industry has such a bustling business. We have so much stuff that we need to rent additional space just to store it. Of course, there are legitimate reasons to rent a storage unit—maybe you are moving and need storage temporarily. However, those reasons are not why the majority of people have items in storage. They have them in storage because they just have far too much and won't get rid of the stuff. If they are honest with themselves, they know they aren't going to use what is in storage. In fact, there is an entire TV show about selling the property in storage units that people have abandoned. That tells me they never needed that storage to begin with.

Regardless of where you are on the scale of having excess stuff, the excess stuff that you have is taking up space in your home, office, car, etc.—space that most people don't have to waste. No one likes living in cramped quarters, much less due to having too much stuff.

ANCHORS

Our things become anchors for us. That can be good or

bad. When one is needing some stability, having our things around us can serve as comfort. I am never as comfortable as when I am in my own home—especially a home that I have literally built and decorated to reflect me and that contains things I love.

However, when we have excess stuff, that stuff becomes an anchor and can literally keep us stuck in a place, when we are meant to move about freely.

Think of it this way. When you travel, especially overseas or for an extended period of time, you definitely want to take enough. However, you don't want to take too much. Why? Because it is a HUGE pain in the ass. Schlepping bags through an airport is not pleasant. I don't care what kind of bag you have. Even if it isn't heavy, it is still a pain in the ass. We have all seen those people with three, four, or five big bags—what is your instant feeling when you see them? OMG—so glad I am not that person. Yes, you want the things that make traveling comfortable and your essentials. But you don't want anything extra.

Just like in traveling, the more stuff you have, the more difficult it is to move around. For those who never want to travel or move from your current home, then fine. But for most of us, we are not in our "forever home." What if an opportunity arose in which you could live for a year in Paris or wherever your favorite place on earth is? Could you easily do that with all of your stuff? Probably not, and the more stuff you have, the more difficult it would be to make that happen.

"Well that opportunity is never going to happen." Maybe, maybe not—but there may be plenty of other reasons you don't want to be shackled by stuff. I had a client once, Julie, who was in a very dangerous domestic violence situation and needed to quickly get herself and her children to safety. Each day, hell, each hour they remained in the home, Julie and her children were in danger. They lived in a 4,000-square-foot home, and she was having a difficult time with the stuff, taking more time than she had to try to pack and take it all. Julie was literally placing herself and her children in danger so that she could pack and take more stuff. Maybe you are not in a horrible situation like that, but being shackled and not free to move is never a good situation.

You are never moving? Really? I have known many an older person who thought they were in their forever home and who later had to move because their home was too much for them to care for, or for health and safety reasons. As one who has had to move her eighty-one-year-old mother across the country, I can tell you sorting through eighty-one years of stuff and moving it isn't fun. If for no other reason than to be kind to your kids, do this work now.

When we have excess stuff—especially a lot of it—it traps

us or at least make it far more difficult to move out of a situation if we need or want to do so.

So, is any of your stuff serving as an anchor for you and your life?

ATTENTION/DISTRACTIONS

Our things demand our attention. There are the obvious ways in which they do so and then very subtle ways of which you may not even be aware. When something is a real problem, it gets our attention quickly. When your home fire alarm is beeping, it has your full, undivided attention. When your car is nearly out of gas, it demands your attention. These situations demand our full attention until the issue is resolved.

Generally, our stuff demands our attention in far more subtle ways, which can be more dangerous and insidious— so subtle that we don't even realize they are calling to us, much less harming us. When we have a lot of stuff cluttering up our lives, or anything cluttering our life, it is very distracting. Our brain is not able to focus on so many things at one time. The best way I can describe this is to give you the grocery store example.

As grocery stores became larger and larger, they increased the number of choices and variety in all goods. If three varieties of jam were good, thirty would be better—right? Customers could find just exactly what they were looking for, with more choices available. Yet, that isn't what happened.

Here is what they found in regard to jelly and jam. In 2000, psychologists Sheena Iyengar and Mark Lepper published a study in which shoppers at an upscale grocery store saw a display table with twenty-four varieties of gourmet jam. If they sampled the jam, they received a coupon for one dollar off any jam. On a separate day, other shoppers were exposed to the same conditions, but with only six jam choices.

Here is what the researchers found: The display with twenty-four jams attracted more interest than the smaller one with only six jams. However, the shoppers in the first group, who had been exposed to the larger display, were only 10 percent as likely to buy jam as the people who were exposed to the smaller display with only six jams.

Other studies confirm the same results, whether it be with other food items or retirement and insurance options. When we are exposed to excessive choice, we don't make any choice. Interestingly enough, even those who do go ahead and choose are less satisfied with their choice, when faced with too many choices.

Choice is good for us, but too much is overwhelming. Each

new choice subtracts a little of our well-being, requires more time and effort, triggers anxiety, and creates unrealistically high expectations and regret if the choice doesn't work out.

You can imagine your own experiment. Just imagine the following situation. It is a hot day and I give you a choice of vanilla ice cream or chocolate ice cream. This is an easy choice for most. You don't have to think about it. You don't have to worry if you made the right decision, and you are happy with the result. In a few seconds, you are feeling the cool, smooth, wonderful ice cream in your mouth and you are happy.

Now, imagine you are hot and I offer you vanilla ice cream or chocolate ice cream. You choose vanilla and I respond:

> French vanilla, Mexican vanilla, Madagascar vanilla, regular vanilla, vanilla swirled with raspberry, vanilla swirled with strawberry, or a combination of any of the two above? What do you want?

Oh my gosh, can you start to feel your anxiety, just reading this?

You are in a no-win situation, no matter what you do. First of all, you have just overloaded your brain. Then no matter which you choose, you are going to wonder if you should have chosen another one. All you wanted was a scoop of freaking ice cream.

So how is a study on jam relevant to your stuff? This is the same process that your brain goes through every time you walk into your closet and have an excessive number of choices to make, every single day—the same process your brain has to go through how many times a day? Which coffee cup do I pick out of the fifty in the cabinet? Which jeans to I wear out of the fifty in the closet? Heck, which chair do I sit in when there are four choices available? So, what do we do? We pick the same cup, the same jeans, and the same chair—day after day after day.

Even more insidious, your brain doesn't even know what to focus on when you are scanning a room with excessive stuff in it. And yes, you do scan it every time you walk in, whether you recognize it or not. It is a safety issue based on our history. We are scanning the room to make sure we are safe. No tigers in the room—okay. Of course, there isn't a tiger in the room—but your body doesn't know that, and it is trying to keep you safe. Just trust me on this and keep reading.

Again, imagine the following two scenes: downtown Las Vegas at night versus the beach. Which makes your eyes literally widen and your heart rate increase, causing you to become hyperalert and sensitive? Not the beach. Your brain is completely overloaded in the Las Vegas scene, as it doesn't know what it is supposed to focus on. There is too much.

Now, I hope your home isn't filled with bright neon signs like the Vegas Strip. However, if it is still cluttered and has a ton of stuff in it (choices for your brain), and your brain is constantly having to decide what to focus on, then it won't focus on anything, or it will keep going to the one choice you make over and over again.

The French have a rule of design in which one or two walls have nothing on them, in order to allow the eye to rest. With too much stuff, your eyes and your brain can never rest.

It might not sound like a big deal, but your brain really does need places to rest.

"But my excess stuff is in a closet or that other room, and I don't see it." So what? Your brain still knows that stuff is all there. Even as you read this last sentence, I bet you could picture what was in the closet. Whether you actually see it or not, your brain is still having to think about it.

ANXIETY

Yes, the more stuff we have, the more we have to worry

about. Most of us have enough in life to worry about without having to worry about our stuff.

I once knew a diamond broker named Levi. He told me the story of a woman who came into his office to get information on selling a diamond ring. The diamond was over thirteen karats (think big-ass, ice cube diamond). This woman had inherited this ring, and it had meant a great deal to her. She wasn't selling the ring because she needed money. She was selling it because since the day she had received the ring, it had caused her nothing but worry, guilt, and grief, even though it was fully insured.

She never wore it, because she worried about it being stolen or falling out of the setting, and she didn't like the attention it received from others. Wearing it was like wearing a neon sign. So, it stayed locked in a safe at her home. And then she felt guilty, as she wasn't enjoying it.

Even though she knew it was "safe," it was always on her mind. Anytime someone was working at her house or she gave a party at the house, she was hyperalert for fear someone might steal the ring.

What was meant to bring her joy was bringing her nothing but worry. She kept the ring for more than two decades, until she had finally had enough. It took her a lot to finally give up the ring, and she had to deal with a lot of internal struggle and guilt in order to do so. When the transaction was complete, she started to cry. The tears were not of regret, but of relief.

What did she do with the money? She went on a trip to the homeland of the family member who had given her the ring. She learned about her history and that of her family. She grew, had fun, and was able to pass on this family history to her own children. In my opinion, that is far more honoring to her family member than keeping the ring in a safe, decade after decade.

Even something not monetarily valuable can cause a lot of worry. Recently, I had to travel from South Dakota to my home in Texas, with my recently deceased father's cowboy hat. This is the *one* thing of my father's that my son, Jonathan, will have to remember his grandfather. I quickly concluded that wearing the hat was the best way to transport it, even though it was too big and I looked ridiculous. It flew off once outside of the airport, and I had to go chasing after it, while wearing a long dress and slip-on shoes. Inside the plane, I put it in the upper storage compartment and worried about it being smashed my entire flight. The flight was a nightmare, due to a tornado, and I got stuck overnight in Denver. What should have been seven hours to get home turned into twenty-four—each one worrying about that damn hat. I forgot it once at security and again had to race back through the airport, going the wrong direction, to retrieve it. I could almost hear my dad roaring with laughter at the scene. I didn't fully relax until that damn hat was at my home, safe and secure.

While that is just one example, we can all think of items that we worry about. Even if not on such a dramatic level or all of the time, our things are still on our minds. The more we have, the more we think about what we have.

A SPECIAL NOTE ON MENTAL HEALTH

I am not a mental health professional in any way. I do have generalized anxiety disorder. While all I have is anecdotal evidence, it is important to note that for me, as well as everyone else I know who has these issues, living in a clutter-free environment is imperative. When one has anxiety or depression, all it takes is one more little thing to push us over the edge. We have enough going on in our heads to deal with, and the last thing we need is to have our brain focus on the stuff in our home, car, or workspace. It can be totally paralyzing.

So if you have anxiety or depression, diagnosed or not, one of the first steps I would recommend, after seeing a professional of course, is to get rid of the extra stuff in your life and make sure that your environment is as clutter-free and calm as humanly possible. If you live with someone who suffers from anxiety or depression, it is imperative that you help, or at least don't hurt, and do your part to keep the space clean and uncluttered. If you don't, you are actually hurting someone else's mental health. I'm serious. It is a big deal. It might just be a pile of laundry to you, but for them it is causing stress and anxiety, or more depression.

FRUSTRATION

When we have excess possessions, it causes frustration. It is frustrating when you can't find what you're looking for, when you have to dig to try and find it. It is frustrating when you can't use your counter, because there is too much stuff on it. It is frustrating when you reach for something and a pile of crap falls down as a result. It is frustrating when others leave their crap all over the house. While certainly not a major life event, who needs more frustration in their life?

NO ROOM FOR WHAT IS REALLY IMPORTANT IN YOUR LIFE

In order to make room for what you really want in your life, you are going to have to make room for it—literally and figuratively. Keeping excess items keeps us stuck, away from what we truly want in life. I can't fully explain it. It is just something you need to experience. When you get rid of the excess stuff, you magically find what you truly want. You think about what you truly want in life. That just doesn't happen before you clear out the old.

Imagine your hands are full of dried beans. You can't eat them as is. They are serving no purpose. Now, imagine a plate of your favorite food in front of you. You can't pick up and eat your favorite food if the beans are still in your hands. You can't have both. You are going to have to let go of the beans (the stuff you don't even want) in order to have what you really want. If your hands are full, there is no room for anything else.

The same goes for your home and your life. Many of us can't have what we really want in life because it's already full of stuff we don't even really care about. If your life is full of stuff that doesn't matter—hell, that you don't even like half the time—there is literally not room for items you will use and enjoy and that will serve you.

A good example of this is clothing. I have never owned even half the clothing that a typical woman in the US has. However, much of what I did have consisted of things I didn't love or that didn't fit me. Only when I got rid of the excess, and the items of clothing that were not serving me, did I have the space, literally and in my head, to really examine what clothes I truly wanted to wear. What clothing made me feel amazing? I ended up with a small wardrobe that I love. That wouldn't have happened without wiping the slate clean.

THE ENVIRONMENT

This book is not about the environment or climate change. It goes without saying, though, that the more one buys and keeps, the more waste is produced. Everything that we own had to be produced, which takes energy and creates waste.

It had to be transported to us or to the store. That takes energy and vehicles. Most of what we buy has packaging, and with some stores or websites, a lot of packaging. That all has to go somewhere. Even if you recycle it, that still takes a lot of energy and resources.

The less one buys, the less one is affecting the environment and wasting resources.

DEMORALIZATION/INTEGRITY/SELF-RESPECT

Many of us know that we have too much stuff. We may not fully appreciate just how much the actual cost is to us, but if we are really honest with ourselves, we know it is too much. So, we get motivated and start to get rid of stuff. Some have so much that it is overwhelming to begin to even *think* about taking care of the problem, so we don't even begin. Others start, feel great, and make a bit of progress, and then life starts up again and they stop. The area they worked on is eventually taken over by too much stuff, slowly and quietly.

What is worse is when we get rid of stuff, only to buy the same or similar back again. Ask me how I know. My best example of this rather insane behavior is my madeleine pans. Madeleines are a specifically shaped little French cake. I don't even love them as a dessert. That didn't stop me from buying the pans twice. My first trip to Paris, I went to the most amazing shop for professional bakers and cooks, called E.Dehillerin. If you have an issue with kitchen stuff, DO NOT go there until you finish this book. Anyway, I bought a madeleine pan, among various other items. And of course, I had to get it home. Yes, I brought a large baking pan from Paris to Seattle. At home, I bought a madeleine cookbook to add to my cookbook collection—despite the fact that I had madeleine recipes in at least two other cookbooks I already owned. I made madeleines once. A few years went by, and I realized that I really wasn't going to use the pan again, so I got rid of it and the cookbook. Within two years, somehow, I had talked myself into buying another madeleine pan, just in case. I am not kidding.

How many times have you done something like that? You wake up to find another 200 pairs of shoes in your closet, or your garage full enough that you can't park your car in it again. This is generally the cycle that we go through when we are trying to simplify. Trying to organize. Trying to get our life together.

Then we feel like failures. We did it again. We said we wouldn't get here again, and here we are. We lied to ourselves. That is completely demoralizing, and we lose self-respect every single time we repeat the cycle. We can't trust ourselves. If you can't trust yourself, then who in the world can you trust and how could anyone else trust you?

This is the real issue. It grates at you little by little. Then the voices start...and they are not kind. "Fuck...I did it again." "I can't believe I just bought that." "I don't even have room for it." And then we defend ourselves and come up with ways to rationalize what we just brought home. We are smart; we can rationalize nearly anything. "I need to look good for my job." "I deserved a treat." "It was only X amount." WHATEVER. The more you feel the need to defend your choice by rationalizing, the fuller of BS you probably are. When an item truly serves us, we don't need to rationalize buying or having it. When we catch ourselves lying to ourselves, it feels horrible, absolutely horrible—so horrible that we continually rationalize in order to avoid facing the truth and feeling the feelings.

The price we pay for having excess stuff is far more than just money. Our excess stuff is affecting us more than we realize and, for some people, it is actually ruining their life.

Thankfully, in chapter 4, you will begin to see why we do this, and in chapter 5, how to stop the cycle forever. But before we continue, think about—better yet, write down—all of the ways in which having too much stuff has negatively affected you. What is your butter curler story? When have you had financial difficulties but also a ton of stuff? When have you behaved in a way you aren't really proud of with regard to stuff? When has stuff caused strife in your marriage or relationships? Take your time, and know that it may sting a bit. Above all, be honest—but no shaming yourself. No one is going to look at this work, and you can only change what you acknowledge.

THE WORK

1. When did you first have excess stuff?
2. How do you feel when you obtain excess stuff?
3. What has excess stuff cost you? Please be thorough, honest, and specific—not just in terms of money but also time, space, and energy.
4. How does it feel to honestly acknowledge what the excess stuff has cost you?
5. What benefits did you think you were getting by having excess stuff? For example, maybe you were distracting from feelings or feeding your ego. What is your "why" for having excess stuff? Again, be honest.
6. How does it feel to know your "why?"

CHAPTER 4

WHY IS IT SO HARD TO GET RID OF OUR STUFF?

"The first step to getting what you want is having the courage to get rid of what you don't."

—UNKNOWN

I looked at the antique photos with resentment. I had long ago forgotten which great-great-grandparents were in the photo, but I "had" to carry them with me during three moves, store them, and care for them for over two decades. Same went for the thirty pieces of crystal stemware that I never used. I wanted it all gone. But how was it not disrespectful to my family, my heritage, and my ancestors, as well as a total act of disloyalty, to get rid of their crap—including the only photos of them in the entire world?

Getting rid of your stuff is far more complicated than just throwing stuff out or giving it away. The process of eliminating the stuff that isn't good for your life will not work until you first do some deep work. This is the key. This is why you have filled up your house over and over and over again after you have gotten rid of stuff. This is probably why every other book, video, and method has failed you in the past.

This chapter is not the "how to" for getting rid of your stuff. Again, don't start purging your things yet. You are starting your work, even if it doesn't feel like it. This chapter briefly touches the most common reasons why people have such a difficult time getting rid of things that don't serve them anymore. Chapters 3 and 4 are closely related, and there is some overlap between the two.

There are many reasons why we have gotten into this position of having too much stuff. They are far more complex than just the fact that we bought too much stuff or live in a larger home than works for us. Until you can see those issues and address them, it won't matter how many times you purge your stuff. You will always just be repeating the cycle.

The good news is that once you recognize why you are buying, it is relatively easy to stop the process. It isn't instant, and it will take some practice, but the more you change your thoughts and behavior, the easier it will be.

You will come to the point of not even wanting the stuff. Seriously.

Neither this book nor this chapter is meant to address individuals with severe mental illness that manifests as extreme hoarding. That is way above my pay grade. If someone you know is an actual hoarder and their life, children, safety, or home is in actual jeopardy, then please stop reading this book and find help from a mental health professional who specializes in hoarding.

There are as many different reasons for keeping things as there are people. However, there are some common themes among many people. Those themes revolve around guilt, fear, ego, and being overwhelmed.

COMFORT AND PERCEIVED SECURITY

"I just feel better having a lot of clothes—it is 'my thing,'" was what one woman, Sarah, said to me when she got even more clothing, even though her other three closets were already full. For many, having lots of stuff provides a sense of comfort or security. It just *feels* better to have a lot of things. Much like a security blanket for a small child, our stuff becomes our adult version. The problem is that you are not a small child anymore. Relying on material possessions, or 2,000 of them, to give you any sense of security is a very false security. It isn't real. There is absolutely no security in having a bunch of stuff—in fact, quite the opposite. You are relying on something outside of yourself to make you feel a certain way, and that is always going to be a losing proposition.

Your sense of self, self-worth, or security is not in some inanimate object, but within yourself. You don't need that security blanket—really. You are giving that object a job that it was never intended to do. That lamp is supposed to supply light and maybe look nice. It isn't supposed to make you feel secure or happy. Those items of clothing are meant to cover you up, keep you warm, and maybe make you feel fabulous wearing them—as an extension of you. They are not meant to be your security or define who you are.

Also, do you really want "your thing" to be that you collect a bunch of stuff? You want your thing, what you are known for, what you spend your time on, to be objects? Why? If so, that might be something you want to examine closely. Are you collecting for the sake of collecting or for some other reason? What is the feeling you are trying to get from collecting an object? Does the object have a purpose? If so, what is that purpose? Or is your purpose to own "a collection" of X? If so, what feeling are you really going after? Why would you want your "thing" to be about a material item?

Especially with this issue, it is going to take some time,

silence, and going deep to see where that need for security is coming from. Even if you cognitively know where it stems from (such as neglect in childhood or other trauma), just knowing isn't enough. You are going to have to feel the feelings again and work through the feelings, not just the thoughts, to move through this issue and be able to move on.

I know this sounds ridiculous, but it works. It has worked for me and others who I have worked with and who have done this exercise. If you suffered trauma as a child (and yes, neglect is trauma), that child is still there and your subconscious doesn't know that you are safe. And make no mistake, your subconscious is in control. So, until it knows it is safe, you are going to continue to do things that aren't really in your best interest now.

How do you tell your subconscious it is safe? By doing just that. When I first heard about this exercise, I rolled my eyes. But I trusted the man who was telling me to do it, so I did it—and wow, it was powerful.

Take time by yourself when you will not be interrupted, and where you have the space to feel, think, cry, etc. Do not try doing this on your lunch hour at work. Think in the forest, on the beach, by yourself in your house. Take out a photograph of yourself as a child—around the time when whatever bad thing was happening. Look at the photo for a good ten minutes. Then, start writing down or recording the thoughts and feelings that bubble up. No judgment, just observations. When you have written down your thoughts and more importantly, your feelings, I want you to talk to that boy or girl in the photo.

Talk to him or her as you would if you were walking into that scene now, as an adult. Tell her she is safe; you will always take care of her. Tell her about what you are doing now and how you can always provide for her. Tell her that she doesn't ever have to worry about having anything. You will protect her. You will provide for her. You will love her. Tell her that her security is within her/you and that she never needs to worry about anything.

This is an exercise that is ongoing. Continue to talk to yourself. When the feelings of fear, scarcity, etc. start coming up, talk to yourself and tell yourself you are okay—again, kindly and without judgment.

You may have to do this exercise a few times in order for things to be released. The first time I did it, I felt good about it, but nothing monumental. The second time I did it, I moved the age to the worst time in my life, when I was thirteen and fourteen, and the floodgates opened. I bawled, just bawled and realized that I had been so mean to myself and had not only accepted other people's shame but had also added to it. I realized that I had been desperately running from myself and had just been horrible to this little fourteen-year-old girl who was scared to death, traumatized, and hurt.

When I got that—for the first time ever—things shifted, and very quickly. It isn't a pleasant experience as you are bringing up a lot of bad feelings, many of which you have stuffed down for years, even decades, but sit tight and work through it. You are an adult and can handle this now. But you have to feel it to get through it.

Doing the heart work is what is going to make the difference in being able to easily get rid of what doesn't serve you and never going back to having too much stuff.

GUILT

When we feel we need to keep other people's things, or items that we have been given by others, it's generally because of guilt. When we are given something, whether it is an inheritance or a gift for us specifically, we feel obligated to keep it. We don't want to hurt the giver's feelings or look ungrateful or disrespectful. And people can get their feelings bent out of shape if we get rid of things.

I have had that very unpleasant experience—the only time my dad was really upset with me—when I gave away family furniture. I really didn't need it, but it *was* beautiful and meant a lot to me. However, it was a lot of furniture, was in a set, and was taking up a lot of room. I also knew another family member would really love to have the set, would appreciate it more, and would take great care of it. I could always get the set back if I wanted it. So, she got the set. I checked with my dad and thought it was fine, but it wasn't. Wires were crossed, communication wasn't as great as it could have been, and holy crap was there fallout.

The decision to part with the furniture was a good one, but my communication about it should have been far clearer. I hurt my dad's feelings, which I never wanted to do.

If I had the chance to do it again, I would be far clearer in my communication, explaining to my dad what it meant for him to give me the furniture, how much I appreciated it, and that given my current living situation, I would have to put it into storage and didn't want to risk it getting damaged. How about we let X family member have it? That way, my dad would have felt he had some control over the situation, and hopefully there wouldn't have been any hurt feelings.

If your relatives are dead, there is NO reason for you to feel any guilt over getting rid of their stuff. You can ask other family members if they want it, which most won't, and then get rid of it. You are under no obligation to keep someone else's property. If they wanted it so badly, they should have taken it with them.

You are not being disrespectful or marring their memory in any way, even if they saved this special item specifically for you. Someone else could be using this item today and getting enjoyment out of it, rather than it sitting on a shelf in your house year after year.

It took me years—actually, well over a decade—after my mother passed away to give away my aunt's beautiful etched crystal stemware. I had carefully packed it for five moves and cherished it. However, I had only used it once since I inherited it. I really thought about my aunt and what she would have wanted me to do. She was a world traveler. She was independent, worldly, and extremely well-read, and she didn't hang on to unnecessary things. The last thing she would have wanted for me would be to have her crystal create any sort of anchor or impediment to the life I wanted. After I really thought about my aunt, it was easy to give the set to a thrift store that supported a good cause. However, even the lady at the drop-off for the store questioned whether I really wanted to part with the crystal. "I wouldn't give this away if I were you," she said. Talk about an inappropriate guilt trip.

I still have plenty of family heirlooms. I use them. I eat on the fine china, not every day but enough to be able to say I use it. I actually cover up with my grandmother's quilts or display them. So, use it, display it because you love it, or get rid of it. You shouldn't keep anything just because someone gave it to you, even a family heirloom.

What about just regular gifts that you receive? Yes, if someone gives you a gift, say for your birthday, it is polite to keep it for at least a second or two. I am not suggesting tossing it in front of the person who gave it to you. Nor do you need to check with them about regifting it or otherwise getting rid of it.

Depending on the situation, if you really don't want it, get rid of it immediately so you are not thinking about it. It may not be worth the hurt feelings to get rid of it immediately if you are going to see the person who gave it to you, in which case, keep it for a reasonably short period of time, then get rid of it or ask them if they would like it back (unless that would cause hurt or hard feelings—if so, then just get rid of it).

The bottom line is that you have no reason to feel guilty or disrespectful for not wanting to keep something that someone gave you. A gift is supposed to be a gift, not an obligation.

FEAR AND EGO

So much of why we have too much stuff is fear. Fear is like most everything else. A little bit of it, in the appropriate settings, is a good thing. Fear keeps us alive when our little voice tells us to run, even though we haven't seen the tiger yet. A little fear keeps us safe. If fear is used to protect us, that is an amazing gift.

Too much fear, or unrecognized fear, keeps us paralyzed and causes us to make decisions that are really not in our best interests. When I say unrecognized fear, what I mean is just that. We do things, or don't do things, because we are afraid, but we don't see it as fear. We don't see it at all. It is like an invisible wall that keeps us from moving freely. Our fear becomes an invisible prison around us.

I see fear show up a lot with regard to people's stuff.

"What if I need it someday?"

Well, chances are that if you are not currently regularly using it, then you won't in the future, either. If you need it someday, then you can go buy another one—right? Well, that would be a waste, you say. My response is that it is being wasted right now. You are not using it. Someone else could use it today. Someone else could be enjoying this item next week, yet it is sitting here in your drawer or garage.

I will tell you that of all of the thousands of things I have gotten rid of, after using my method properly, I have never *needed* any of them again. The trick is to do the work in chapter 5 so that you won't ever feel that need again.

My father would have this argument with me all the time. He was a contractor and had a lot of tools. He needed those tools for work. He also had a lot of tools and miscellaneous stuff he hadn't used in years, actually decades. He had four storage units, a full garage, stuff on his property, and a shipping container—all full of stuff.

Over the years, with my brothers' help, we managed to winnow it down to three storage containers. I totally got that, of course, my dad needed the tools he used and back-up tools. I got that one might only use that specific tool every two years. My dad was also in a rural area in Montana where he couldn't just go and rent a tool easily.

All of that didn't explain the window, though. My father had bought a very large, expensive window for a home years ago that was never installed. It was dated (think beautiful in 1992), huge, and heavy. But by God, my dad had paid a lot of money for it, it was a *beautiful* window, and it was worth some money. It was worth what someone would pay for it, and in twenty-five years, not a person on the planet had wanted to pay a thing for it. When my dad moved from Chicago to Montana, he took the damn window with him. He stored it for years. It was still in storage when he died.

My father had grown up very poor and, frankly, neglected in many ways. He had been on his own since he was fourteen. Stuff was his security blanket.

So in many cases we, as people, let fear take control, and we keep things that have long since stopped serving us. Ego and fear are very much related.

Ego, in regard to not getting rid of things, comes in the form of consciously or subconsciously thinking that our status will go down if we don't have the item. Yes, there is fear intertwined with ego—that people won't think of us as highly as they do now if we don't have X item. If you move into a smaller home, people will think you are not as wealthy as you want them to believe. If you get rid of your furniture, jewelry, or some of your expensive clothing, people will notice and not hold you in as high esteem. If we get rid of most of our books, how will people automatically know we are highly intelligent?

Most of us don't want to admit that we keep things to impress other people, but we do. The more stuff we have, the more money we have, or at least had at one time. The larger the home we live in, the more money we have, the more successful we are—and we all want to be successful.

Ego, in regard to not letting things go, is just another side of fear. When it comes down to it, we are fearful. We are fearful that our social status will be affected in some way. We are fearful that people won't treat us the same without all of the stuff. We are fearful that people won't respect us or love us without all of the stuff.

OVERWHELMED

Even if we don't have forty years' worth of stuff, it can be completely overwhelming to even think about being able to start going through stuff and begin the process of getting rid of it. So, we don't. We just let it continue to sit and pile up. We tell ourselves that we don't have the time—that we will get to it someday, which is not a day of the week by the way—but deep down, we know we are not going to do it. It is just too overwhelming.

I knew a young lady, Liz, with an anxiety disorder. It was imperative that she get rid of some of her things and get organized so that she could live comfortably—as in get a bed in her room. She was so overwhelmed by the process, by the sheer scale and size of the task before her, that she focused on what she could focus on. That was organizing her pens. To the outsider, this sounds absurd. Why would you organize your pens when you have larger things to do, far more important things, so that you can sleep in a bed? Because at that moment she needed some control. And her pens were all she could handle. That is why. She was completely overwhelmed and doing all she could do.

Years ago, I was helping my mother, who was eighty at the time, move across the country to live closer to me. I had a limited timeframe and a lot to get done. My mother grew up during the Depression and kept anything and everything that could be useful. During this trip, I counted no less than

200 Styrofoam trays (the trays that meat comes in from the grocery store) that she had saved. She would wash and sterilize them, and then use them for storing things. She also had hundreds of bread bags that she would wash and reuse. My mom was an original recycler. Yes, she used them. No, she didn't need the volume of containers or bags she had. She "needed" maybe two or three of each.

At one point, I was getting a bit frustrated with the process and my mother's "delay" in just throwing stuff out. I told her, impatiently, that we had to just start throwing stuff out. Well, much to my shame, later on I found some important family documents in the trash that my mother had thrown out after I snapped at her. She had gotten overwhelmed and just starting throwing stuff out. Yes, I immediately stopped myself and adjusted my attitude, and we got the job done. I would handle the entire situation far differently today, needless to say. Sorry about that, Mom.

When one starts to go through their stuff, it immediately evokes memories and feelings, good and not so good. It is an emotional process. I will teach you how to handle those emotions later on, and it won't be difficult after you learn my method. But be aware that our feelings are real and they can keep us stuck, even when we aren't aware of them.

Disposing of your stuff can also be a pain in the rear. Do not underestimate the sheer amount of time, work, and energy it actually takes to get rid of your stuff. There is the sorting through, taking to the donation site or the trash, and delivering items to others. Selling items can be an even bigger pain in the rear.

Once you go through my method, it will be far easier, mentally and emotionally, to get rid of your extra stuff. It is still going to be a pain in the rear. It will be totally worth it, but still a pain in the ass.

BECAUSE WE ARE "SUPPOSED" TO HAVE IT

We will touch on this subject again later on, but for now know that we have all been taught, by society, that we are supposed to have stuff and want stuff. We are literally given gifts when we are born. Some gifts are gifts that no baby in the world needs. Yet we still give them and receive them. We have cultural norms with regard to the stuff we are "supposed" to own. We are bombarded every single day with message after message about what we should own and buy that day.

Don't underestimate the pressure in this society, in particular, to have things. Beginning to even question the idea of not needing so much stuff in your life is going against the vast majority of the messaging this world gives you every single day. If one is good, ten is better. If a car is good, a larger, more expensive car is better. So yes, there is immense pressure to have the stuff.

YOUR WHY

What is your "why"? Why are you hesitant to part with your excess stuff? What feelings does it bring up to think about taking the time to go through your stuff and purge the excess? What do you hear yourself saying when you think of getting rid of that particular item? Is what you are telling yourself even true? I have done this exercise with myself countless times and with others. Your "why" gets to the heart of the issue. Keep asking yourself why you want that item, until you get to the real answer.

THE WORK

1. What, if anything, are you keeping that belongs to someone else?
2. What are you keeping out of a feeling of obligation?
3. What are you keeping to impress others?
4. What are you keeping out of a sense of safety or security?
5. Pick a few things that you know are excess and write about why you are keeping those items. Be honest, but don't judge yourself.
6. When you think of getting rid of your excess stuff, do you feel overwhelmed at all? If so, how overwhelmed to you feel, on a scale of one to ten, with ten being "completely paralyzed"?
7. If that feeling of overwhelm is above a six, what would help you overcome that feeling?

8. Write more about any feelings you have about anything that comes up as a result of this chapter.

9. What is your why? Your why for even thinking about examining your relationship with your stuff, or your why for wanting a simpler life? How will your life be better once you only have property that serves you? How will a simpler life be better for you?

{ CHAPTER 5 }

WHY WE BUY SO MUCH STUFF

"Happiness resides not in possessions, and not in gold. Happiness dwells in the soul."

—DEMOCRITUS

Most of the reason we buy things—and *all* of the reason why we buy things we don't really need—is to feel better than we do right now. Many times, we buy because we really don't know what fits us, so we keep trying things on—again, literally and figuratively. Sometimes we buy for necessity. And sometimes we buy and buy and buy, trying to fill a cup that has no bottom. We don't recognize that the cup has no bottom, so we just continually put more into the cup hoping that it will fill up someday and we will feel "good."

STUFF WE NEED

Of course, we buy things we need to simply live and to live comfortably. Those things would include the food that we eat, many household goods, clothing that we wear, furniture we sit on, books we read, and many other items that make our life more comfortable. These are the items we use and items that fit us—who we are, our tastes—and provide us with comfort. These include luxury items as well if they are serving us.

Then there is everything else.

We buy everything else for a variety of reasons, but they all generally fall into the category of ego.

EGO

When I talk of ego, I am not talking about an egomaniac who is full of himself and narcissistic. I am talking about the ego that each and every one of us has. Our ego is the part of us that tells us our self-worth, our value, and who we are is tied to what we do for a living, who we associate with, who we are married to, what stuff we have, how big of a house we own, how many cars we drive, and all of the other external stuff. That ego sparks our fear of not having enough. That ego tells us we don't really need to get rid of stuff; we just need to organize it. That ego keeps us trapped.

Ego is the main reason we buy too much stuff and keep it—stuff we don't need or even really want, for more than a moment in time.

Don't be too hard on yourself; it isn't all your fault. In nearly every society, people demonstrate power, superiority, and ego by displaying wealth. Cleopatra wasn't wearing gold because it felt good on her skin.

We are also under immense and intense pressure to buy, buy, buy in this society. You can't go anywhere without being bombarded with very targeted and well-researched advertising telling you that unless you buy X, no one will love you, you will be a loser, you are a bad mom or dad, and you will die alone. I'm not really exaggerating much here. Marketers spend millions upon millions researching their messages to see what will really hit us and compel us to buy their products.

Even though we know it is all bullshit, we still do it—even the people selling us the shit...and making up shit in order to sell us more shit...and doing that so that *they* can make more money...to buy *their own* shit...that someone *else* is telling them shit to get them to buy. It is nuts. In other words, even the people who are actually manufacturing the bullshit have bought into the bullshit.

COMPARING OURSELVES TO OTHERS

The surest way to drive yourself crazy and feel dissatisfied with your life is to compare yourself to other people, yet we do it all the time.

Let's get something clear right off the bat: there is *always* going to be someone wealthier than you. Prettier than you. Who has a better body than you. If you are continually, or ever, judging yourself or your life by what other people have, you will *never* be satisfied or happy—EVER. This is one of the surest ways to try to fill the cup that has no bottom.

I have seen many people do damage to themselves by trying to keep up with other people. Remember, I have practiced law for over two decades and have seen behind the curtain into people's actual lives, not just their Facebook facades. Years ago, I knew of a woman, Jane, who was the assistant to an incredibly wealthy individual named Susan. Think one of the top five wealthiest persons in the entire world. Jane made a good salary that would comfortably take care of her and her children's reasonable living expenses. She also received lots of free stuff from her employer. However, she was in a world that was not her own, and it wasn't "enough" for her. She continually tried to keep up with Susan. This was absurd. There is no way in hell that Jane was ever going to catch up to Susan or keep up with her. Susan was one of the wealthiest people in the entire world. Yet Jane tried to dress like her, drive an expensive car, and travel to the same places as Susan. Of course, it was never enough. Jane was continually overspending, going into debt, and was really jeopardizing her life by constantly comparing herself to her boss.

Was Jane stupid? Absolutely not. She was highly intelligent but got off course by comparing herself to others.

With the advent of reality TV and social media, this issue is only made worse. Now, instead of comparing ourselves with our peers at work, school, or another social setting, we are comparing ourselves with others all over the world. We want the same handbag that Kate Middleton has. She is a freaking duchess, and we still think we should have the same stuff she has.

When you compare what you have to what others have, no matter what you have, it is never going to be enough. You are always going to need the next thing to make you happy. To make you fit in. To make you feel like you are one of them.

BUYING TO FEEL LIKE AN ADULT

We also buy things because we think "adults" have these things. Adults have big homes. Adults have homes filled with things. Adults have coolers. I remember being in my late twenties and meeting my now-former husband. One of the things I remember about meeting him was that he had three or four good, large ice chest coolers. I remember being impressed with this fact, like he was a real adult. He had the coolers. Adults have coolers. I have to laugh now. Does having a cooler really have anything to do with being an adult? No, but at the time, in my head it did.

It used to make me feel like a real adult, for a few minutes, when I had many sheet sets and towel sets, as I was fully prepared for guests, or when I could have fifty people over to my home for a sit-down dinner easily, with all of the necessary items. We tell ourselves that adults have full sets of tools, household goods, vehicles, sports stuff, and extras. Adults have stuff. If you want to be a real adult, you need stuff.

SECURITY, LONELINESS, OR BOREDOM

This has also been a hot button for me. When I grew up, I thought we were poor. We weren't; we just didn't have a lot of extra stuff. My mom grew up during the Depression, and we didn't waste money on extras or new things, when what we had would do. I left home at nineteen, and my son and I were on our own, with no financial assistance other than student loans, a bit of childcare assistance, and, for a few months, food stamps. I was waiting tables to pay the rent and our bills. Times were tough, real tough, and were for years. We didn't have health insurance. I barely had car insurance. Our monthly grocery budget was ninety dollars a month for two people. I was in complete survival mode. I look back now and still don't know how I did it.

As a result of that time, when I did get a tiny bit more money in law school, I began stockpiling things, especially toiletries and nonperishable food. So, when I would get a student loan check, I would get extra items to make sure we would never run out. Even if the money ran out, at the least we would have food in the cupboards.

However, this behavior continued and only grew worse, even well after I was out of school and doing more than surviving. I still had this scarcity mentality and would keep ridiculous amounts of toiletries, paper goods, and nonperishable food to make sure we never ran out.

It isn't uncommon for people who have lived in poverty, or close to it, to stockpile items, even to the point of financially harming themselves. It would seem intuitive that if one had been poor, one would save money and not buy items they didn't need, but I can tell you that is not the case.

Having stuff can make one feel more secure. Having excess stuff can make one feel more "normal." Depending on the situation, of course, poverty can cause trauma. That trauma is strong and makes us do things that aren't always in our best interest, just to make us feel more secure.

KIDS

Man, do we buy a lot of stuff for our kids. Yes, kids do require a lot. Even newborns require a lot: car seats, bassinets, diapers, clothing, special cleansers, lotions, and even special detergents, books, toys, strollers...OMG.

Of course, we need to buy things for our kids. They need items to keep them safe and comfortable. Do they need or even want all of what they have, though? I have known some pretty poor families, who had very little, and still had way too much stuff for their kids. I have been to children's birthday parties or Christmases where the sheer volume of gifts they received pushed them into a total meltdown because it was overwhelming.

I get it. Kids need stuff. We want our kids to have things. We don't want our kids to feel left out or be made fun of because they don't have what other kids have. I have been the kid who was made fun of for not having cool stuff. I have also been the single mom who couldn't afford to buy her son much of the cool stuff.

I felt so much guilt about not being able to buy him lots of books or toys or to take amazing vacations. I had no guilt about not being able to buy him video games, which I didn't want him to have in the first place. When he joined Boy Scouts, it took me months to afford the uniform. Each week, I felt like crap dropping him off at his meeting without having a uniform, and I felt such pride when the week came when he could wear his uniform to his Boy Scout meeting.

We *so* want for our children. We want them to have the best possible life. And we can want so much for them that we overload them. When we overload them with stuff, they can't focus on anything or appreciate what they have. Just like the jam—too many choices cause them to walk away from everything.

GIFTS

To show love and hope to get it in return—I love gifts. I love giving gifts, and I love getting gifts.

It is somewhat easy to overbuy in order to show people we love them. Many of us go overboard on the number of things we buy for other people or the expense. Gifts are one way in which we can show people that we love them.

I certainly have given gifts I could absolutely not afford to people I loved. I can tell you that the people who love you would never want you to give them anything that caused you financial stress. Harming yourself is not a healthy way to show love to anyone else. What we are really doing is making a rather desperate (sorry, that one hurt didn't it?) attempt to get people to love us or love us more.

Many times, it is not a conscious thought pattern, but the thinking is "If I get them this, they will know just how much I really love them and will love me in return." This happens more than we like to admit. Alternatively, sometimes we give gifts in the hope of getting a gift in return. That isn't really even a gift, is it?

Before automatically giving someone stuff, ask yourself: Do the people you are giving gifts to need anything? Do they even want anything? Or are you just adding to their crap pile and giving them the stress and added work of having to store something or get rid of it?

Absent the people I know needing something, I just give people consumable gifts—something I know that they will use and that is special, like hand-pressed olive oil from Italy, handmade soap, or something I bake.

So, the next time you are tempted to give a gift for any reason other than just out of the generosity of your heart, take a step back and think about why you are giving it.

TO FIT IN, FEEL NORMAL, AND FEEL WORTHY

Many of us grew up in a poor family, or at least compared to those around us. That was me. No, we were never poor. I always had all of my needs met. We owned a modest home, always had plenty of food, never had to worry about the lights being turned off, and we traveled. None of that mattered to me though when I was eight. My mother had grown up during the Depression. Stuff wasn't important to her. She also didn't have a high income. She completely had the philosophy of "wear it out, use what you have, or do without." She never had any debt, other than our home. We always had emergency savings and were financially safe and secure. I can appreciate all of those amazing financial habits now that I am an adult. However, at the time, it sucked.

And I had the same ugly lunch box my entire elementary school career. I had a mixture of store-bought clothes and clothes my mother had made for me. I had plenty of toys, but not compared to my friends. Our car was old, and I so longed for a new car. We only had "real" Froot Loops on special occasions. On regular days, we had generic cereal. This was the 1970s and 1980s. I don't know if generic food has improved, but at that time it sucked. Totally sucked.

I don't have a specific memory of being teased for not having the cool stuff, but I sure felt it. All I wanted was to be "normal." To have a "normal" house that had nice furniture in it. Not to be embarrassed by our car, clothes, or other stuff.

We all want to be a part of the tribe, as we are social creatures. We don't want to be ostracized from the tribe because of what we don't have. I get it—I totally get it. And buying things to fit in isn't completely bad. It does serve a purpose—to a point. A certain level of stuff does help us fit in, or at least not stand out from the crowd. However, if you think that buying stuff is ever going to eradicate the feeling of not belonging, I fear you are in for a long ride. I have talked to many people in similar situations and they never got over it, until they did the hard work—soul-searching to get to the feelings and then dealing with them. It doesn't matter what you wear or what you drive; you never truly feel like you are one of them. And that is okay. We all have our issues. Guess what? They probably don't feel like they fit in, either. We all have imposter syndrome. The people you are still trying to fit in with have their own issues—believe me.

CHASING THE HIGH

When we buy something, many times we do get a high from it. I have driven off of the car lot in a beautiful Mercedes. It felt amazing. I was on top of the world. It felt great, for maybe a week, just like any time we get something great. It doesn't matter what it is—the high doesn't last. I still had a great car that I enjoyed driving, but that initial high was gone. So, what do we do? We buy the next thing to get that high again. We get addicted to the high. There are many people who are so addicted to that high that they use shopping as an activity in and of itself, like a sport, something to entertain them.

They have item after item of clothing with the tags still on it, or still in bags. Many times, they have so much stuff, they don't even really know all of what they have. They shop to "relax." They shop "to see what new things are out." They shop to get the high.

Again, it isn't about the stuff. It is about the feelings. Then we feel like we have too much and know that it isn't good for us. Until you deal with the feelings you were trying to chase or bury when you were buying the stuff, you will always struggle with the stuff. You deal with the feelings by feeling them, journaling about them, and acknowledging them.

Until you know that your self-worth, your value, is not in any way tied to your stuff, you will continue to buy or get the stuff in order to make yourself feel better, to try to make yourself feel more valuable and more loveable. When you know your self-worth, when you know it has nothing to do with the stuff you own, *then, and only then,* are you not continually feeling the urge to buy more stuff.

The good news is that once you do let go, it removes the need to chase the high. It removes the wanting, the pining, the desire for stuff that doesn't serve you. You can look at all of the stuff that used to make you twitch, and easily and casually say, "No, thanks," without even a second glance.

You are no longer trying to fill the cup that has no bottom.

For me, I was only able to do this honest self-examination and let go of my ego at one of my lowest life moments. I had left a home that I loved and a practice, and moved across the country to rural Texas in order to simplify my life, live debt-free, and take care of my dad. Yet that isn't what happened. What happened was that I ended up in a beautiful, fully furnished, renovated farmhouse that was larger than I needed or wanted, with a 2.3-acre yard that was a huge pain to take care of, and in a lot of debt, battling scorpions, snakes, and fire ants on a regular basis.

I had a $7,000 lawnmower, but nothing left in the bank. I had an $8,000 gas range and didn't know how I was going to pay the bills next month. I was totally broke. I had worked so hard, yet I was in this same stuck place again with too much stuff and still broke. I had a choice at that moment. I could do my normal (that is to place at least some blame elsewhere), or I could take the punch and take 100 percent responsibility and fix this, once and for all.

I had a problem, and it was my problem to fix.

We each have our little voice, gut, soul, whatever you want to call it. It knows the truth and will never steer us in the wrong direction. But one has to be very quiet and still in order to hear that voice. The more I sat and was quiet, the louder my little voice became. I started becoming compelled—and that is the only word to describe it—to get rid of stuff. And given what I had already left in Seattle before the move, I didn't think I had much to get rid of, but I did.

I went through my clothing again, things I had just bought because they were Texas style and I was now a Texan. They weren't me. More clothing, more house goods, tools, and materials from the house renovation. I even got rid of family heirlooms and crystal.

I didn't really understand what was happening at the time, but I knew I needed to just go with it. I also knew that I was at a crossroads in my life. I was so frustrated, confused, and demoralized. I was smart, creative, and hard-working. How had I allowed having too much stuff and no money to happen—again?

It was then that I gave up my ego. I finally realized that it was my ego that had gotten me to this place and that in order for me to really make changes in my life—to really simplify my life and get peace—I was going to have to tell my ego to fuck off. I was ready. I was ready to do whatever I needed to do in order to get peace in my life and peace in my head. I was worthy of peace.

I began to think about what I really wanted. Not what I was *supposed* to want, but what I *really* wanted. Not what my family would want or what other people would think, but what *I* wanted.

I wanted simplicity. The more I thought about what I wanted, the more I knew it wasn't what everyone else wanted or what I had been told I should want. I didn't want a big house or a big yard. I didn't want my calendar to be packed full. I didn't even want to entertain anymore.

As the process continued in my head, I knew that I was going to have to face the big, ugly truth. I didn't want my house. I didn't want 2.3 acres. I didn't want what I had just spent the last year and every last penny to my name, plus a lot of debt, to build.

I had just fucking bought it. I had just spent the last nine months working twelve-hour days fixing and decorating it. I had just gone through the hell of renovation. I really couldn't believe it myself. I knew what needed to be done, and crap, no one was going to understand. I was going to take so much flak for this one.

But I knew, I just knew, that I had to regroup, to get as small as I could to really focus and get my foundation solid. I wasn't giving up on owning my dream home. It would be there—just not today. I just needed to retreat and regroup. My ego was going to have to sit this one out.

So, I sold my home. It closed on the same week I had bought it a year before. And I got rid of nearly everything. I wasn't moving things that didn't serve me or support me,

AGAIN. If I didn't use it regularly, if it didn't serve me, if I didn't love it, if I had it to impress anyone, even a little bit, it was gone.

With every trip to the thrift store, I felt lighter. I felt more like myself. I felt free. I still didn't know exactly what my future looked like, but I knew it didn't include a bunch of stuff.

My process of simplifying continued as it spread like light. I started thinking more and more about my law firm. I really didn't need a physical office, given the amazing shared workspaces available. That meant I didn't need all of the stuff in my office, either. So, I moved out of the physical office where I'd been working and got rid of more stuff.

Shortly after the first of the year, I was down to living and working in a nice apartment, with only things that I used, that I loved, and that supported me. I didn't have extras. I didn't have "just in case" or "may use someday" items. Everything had a purpose, even if that purpose was just to give me joy and a shot of beauty or invoke a good memory.

I didn't feel the need to justify or defend anything I owned anymore. I knew that what I had was right for me, and I didn't have one extra thing that was serving to weigh me down, distract me, or cause me stress. I was free. Everything I had served me, not the other way around.

The path to get here wasn't easy or fun. Growth is not easy. Growth is painful. Many people don't understand others' growth, and it can look really messy. And it is the only way to get to the other side.

THE WORK

1. What excess stuff do you have that you purchased as a result of trying to impress others?
2. What excess stuff do you have that you purchased because you thought you would feel better, successful, wealthy, more attractive, etc. with it?
3. What excess stuff do you have that you purchased to make yourself feel more secure?
4. What excess stuff do you have that you purchased when you began to compare yourself to other people?
5. How often do you compare yourself to other people?
6. How do you feel when you compare yourself to other people?
7. What stuff have you purchased because it made you feel like "an adult"?
8. What are your habits in regard to gift giving? Do you go overboard? Have you ever given a gift you couldn't really afford? Have you ever felt resentment when you gave a gift? What are you really trying to get when you give gifts?
9. Have you purged before, only to rebuy the same or similar items?

10. Why do you continue to purchase items that you don't need or love? Be honest and go deep. That is where the magic happens.

{ CHAPTER 6 }

WHAT THE HELL DO YOU WANT?

"You show your worth by what you seek."

—RUMI

Of course, everyone wants a big, beautifully furnished home with a pool and a new luxury car, to be able to go on two amazing vacations per year, and to have a wardrobe that could be in a magazine spread. Isn't that the "American Dream"?

You can't live with the purpose of having only things that serve you if you don't know what you really want in the first place. What we really want is a life and possessions that fit us intellectually, physically, emotionally, socially, and spiritually. It doesn't matter if something is pretty, cute, cool, or amazing if it isn't you. There can be a really big difference between what we actually want and what we are *supposed* to want.

This isn't about what you want versus what you need, either. If you really want to get down to it, all you really need is a bit of shelter, water, and enough food to keep you alive every day. Yet I don't know about you, but that isn't how I want to live. I trust that isn't how you want to live, either. So instead of phrasing in terms of "want versus need" let's think in terms of "Does this fit you, and is it what you want in your life?"

What we are *supposed* to want is easy to recognize. We are told 10,000 times a day what we should want. We are supposed to want to make a lot of money, millions if we can. We are supposed to want a home that is at least 3,500 square feet, and better if it is over 7,000 square feet. We are supposed to want a second home on the beach or in the mountains and all of our homes beautifully decorated, along with all of the things we see advertised to us. At the very least, we should have nice, new clothing each year and a new car every three years.

We are always *supposed* to want more. Even if your income and lifestyle are fairly modest, you are still supposed to want more. Into crafts? Great, here is the newest, latest gadget or tool that you *need* for your craft. Never mind that you have been crafting just fine for twenty years, wonderfully, without this latest gizmo.

Whatever we have is not enough. It isn't good enough. You now need this lotion in order to take care of your skin properly. You need this device to see if you are running properly. Ignore last year's device that promised the same thing—you need this year's device.

Don't even get me started on computers and smartphones that are out of date by the time you get them home.

We are continually sold the shiny ball of shit. All of the time.

Here is the problem—well, one of them. The chair may be too big or too small. Remember *Goldilocks and the Three Bears*? One chair was too big, one chair was too small, and one chair was just right. We are continually told that we should want the big chair. But what if that big chair doesn't fit us?

The big homes, the flashy cars, and the shiny balls of shit may look great from the outside. It may be tempting to think we want them, and if only we could make the money to get that shiny ball, we would be happy. But is it even what you want? Does it fit your life and you?

A large component of a simple life is knowing who you are—

not who you are *supposed* to be. Know what you like and don't like—not what you are *supposed* to like or not.

I lived in the Pacific Northwest for over twenty years and in Seattle for nearly a decade of that time. I had fully renovated my home, and it was lovely and very me. I lived close to downtown, had a view of the water and city, and had a great life. Anywhere I would travel, people would ask where I lived. The immediate response when I said Seattle was "Oh, I love Seattle." I get it. Seattle is a great city. And I was *supposed* to love it far more than I did. The more I stripped down and got real with who I was and what I wanted, the less I wanted Seattle. I wanted sun. I didn't want traffic and such a fast-paced growth. There were other things about living there that just were not for me anymore. At one time they were and Seattle worked for me. Not anymore. So just because other people think something is great doesn't mean you have to.

We are all individuals. We all have different tastes and preferences. Living simply and superbly means that we only have what fits us, regardless of what others say we should like. I do not like fish or coffee. You would be amazed by what strong opinions others had in Seattle about the fact that I didn't like salmon or coffee. Some people thought it was bizarre. Many people tried to convince me that I was just wrong—that I had just not tasted the right salmon or coffee, and if I did, I would love it. Some people actually got a little agitated. It was so strange to me. Why would anyone else care if I liked or didn't like salmon or coffee?

Regardless of your tastes, as long as they aren't immoral, what you like or don't like is totally fine. Some people like the color orange; others don't. It is okay not to like the color orange. Some people like living in the city, and others like living in the country. Both are fine. Some people don't want to worry about getting the latest gadget every year and are actually more comfortable in a small apartment rather than owning a home. Whatever your taste is, that is okay, and you don't need to defend it to anyone. What you do need is to know your own taste in order to only have possessions in your life that fit your taste.

You can also appreciate something and find it beautiful without actually wanting to own it. For instance, I can fully appreciate the beauty of many cars. That doesn't mean I want to own one. I can appreciate how lovely a Ferrari is and the craftmanship contained in each one, yet I never want to own a Ferrari. I don't want to maintain it, protect it, pay for it, or frankly with my claustrophobia, even want to get in one.

I can appreciate a beautifully decorated log cabin and still know that log cabins are not me, and I would not be comfortable staying in one for more than a short time. They just aren't me. There is no judgment here; it is just knowing what you like and don't like.

Part of what is you, what fits you, may be not owning a lot of stuff or having a complex life.

So, one of the most important things you will do in your journey to simplify is to dig deep and figure out what you *really* want, not what you are *supposed* to want. These answers generally only come to people when their mind is quiet—when there are not interruptions, stimulations, and a bunch of other stuff going on.

If money were no object and you could have your dream home, anywhere in the world, your dream car, your dream possessions, your dream life, what would it look like? What would you own? Do you really want a mansion, or honestly do you really want just a fabulous home that works for you and that totally fits you? Do you really want a Ferrari, or does a Volvo fit you better? Do you want all the new gadgets every six months, or does that actually bring you some anxiety?

These are not brain questions but soul, heart, and gut questions. Where do you feel most at home? Where do you feel most comfortable? Where do you feel most you? What is "you"?

Perhaps some examples will help. One of the most important categories to know thyself is in our clothing, as we literally put it on our bodies every single day. I feel most me in comfortable clothing from France. If I can get items in thrift stores there, all the better. I know that is really specific and odd. I love French fashion. I don't know why; it is just me. I feel more comfortable in it than any other clothing (excluding yoga pants, of course).

Likewise, I don't want a big house. I am not comfortable in a big house, just like I wouldn't be comfortable in a tiny house. Even if it is perfectly tidy, money isn't an issue, help isn't an issue—it just isn't me. It took me a long time to get to this point, as a big house is what you are supposed to want. You are supposed to want to be rich, and when you get rich, you get a mansion, or at least a really big house—the bigger the better. All rich people have big homes, right?

I would go to other people's homes, and some mansions, and they were lovely. For twenty seconds, I would fantasize about living in them, but it never felt right. It always felt too big. When I got to the point of really listening to myself, I realized I didn't want that. I didn't want big. It didn't fit me.

However, too small a home might not fit either. I am very claustrophobic, and I work out of my home. If I tried to live in a home under 800 square feet, much less a tiny home, I would lose my mind. So again, it is about what fits you—not anyone else.

Even with money, we are always supposed to want more

and more of it. Now, there is the whole abundance mindset that is even taught in churches. What if you don't really want that much money? What if you just want enough money to do what you want to do, meet your needs, and give? What if you get that after your basic needs are met, happiness doesn't improve with money?

To thine own self be true—always. But you have to get real with yourself, be totally honest, and think about what you really want. What makes you smile to think about it? Where would you feel nurtured? Where and under what circumstances do you feel most you? Look at pictures of different homes, clothing, décor, and cars. What makes you feel the most comfortable? What is "you"? Notice how you feel. Is it a "hell yes"? If not, it probably isn't for you.

And it is okay if "you" is completely eccentric. I sure am. At any time in my home, you will see French antiques, mid-century modern, American folk, Swedish, and desert chic all at the same time, and it works—for me. Living in a matchy-matchy home or one with only one style isn't me.

You can also experiment and see how you like things.

One of the huge benefits of figuring out what you really want is it gives you freedom, relieves a lot of pressure, and gives you focus. This is especially true if you figure out that you don't really want all of the shiny balls of shit. A whole lot of pressure is instantly gone. If you figure out what you really want—what will feed your soul and nurture you—and it turns out that it is a lot less than you thought, you just freed up a whole lot of money and time. Your finish line just got a lot closer to you.

Keep in mind that getting to what you really want is a process. It is like taking away layers of an onion. It will take time. Just keep at it.

If you are reading this, I suspect that you, the real you, is simpler than you may think and is wanting simplicity over complexity. Part of this questioning, of course, is to examine what you think your purpose in this life is—no small question or task. No, you don't have to know the answer in order to simplify your life. I don't know what your purpose is, but I know what it isn't. No one's purpose is to continually buy and collect stuff. It doesn't matter what that stuff is. It isn't your purpose to amass huge sums of money and keep it. It isn't your purpose to amass collections of homes, cars, clothes, or any other item. No, the one with the most toys when he dies doesn't *win*.

Also know that we go through stages in our lives, and what fits you can change. What you once wanted you may not now, and that is perfectly fine. Again, at one time I loved to entertain. Some of that was ego and some was me. As I grew into my mid- and late forties, I just didn't want to do it anymore. A small gathering is fine, but not the large parties I used to throw. When I was really honest with myself and concluded I didn't want to entertain like that anymore, I felt instant relief. Entertaining had been a fun part of my life, and now it was time to move on.

This also meant I could get rid of a ton of stuff. At least half or more of my kitchen stuff was for entertaining. Even after many purges, I had lots of different glassware, dish sets, outdoor sets, trays, serving dishes, etc. And furniture. Entertaining takes a lot of stuff. All of that could now go.

Will I entertain in the future? I don't know. Certainly not like I did at one time. And if I ever have the need for additional dishes and things, I will borrow them for the evening, not go and buy the entire entertainment section of a store.

So give yourself permission to change what you want if it no longer serves you.

TAKING 100 PERCENT RESPONSIBILITY

In order for you to get full control—or any control for that matter—of your stuff, you must take 100 percent responsibility. It can be confusing what that means, as there is a very fine line between taking responsibility and taking blame. In its simplest terms, taking 100 percent responsibility means that if you have a problem, it is your problem to fix. It doesn't matter who created the problem. So yes, others may be to blame, or at least somewhat to blame, for whatever situation you are in. They may have hit your car, may have dropped the ball at work, may have hurt you, whatever, but if you have a problem, it is your problem to solve. That is taking 100 percent responsibility.

Why in the world take full, 100 percent responsibility when it wasn't all, or in some cases any, of your fault? Because that is the *only* way to fix the problem that you are having.

No one wants to admit that they don't take responsibility for fixing their life. No one wants to admit they act like a victim—which is exactly what one is doing when one doesn't take 100 percent responsibility for their life. So, I will start. I used to have a rather large issue with not taking 100 percent responsibility for my life. It took a lot of work to be able to see the line between blaming others and taking full responsibility. The truth is I didn't feel like a victim, but I was blaming everyone else for my problems. If only my clients would pay me. I could be happy if my husband would stop drinking. If only I could get more clients. If only there weren't chips in the house, then I wouldn't eat them. If only my kids would behave. If only other people would pick up their messes. I would go for a run, if only it weren't raining or cold, or hot. If only...

I started doing some really hard internal work and fully

accepting that regardless of why something had happened to me and regardless of who else was involved or not, if I had a problem, it was my problem to fix. It wasn't until then that life began to get better. It certainly wasn't overnight, and it took a lot of practice, but it worked. It is easier to blame other people and not take action. However, that is never going to fix the problem. You have to do things you don't want to do—and a lot of them for a long time. And it is the only way to fix the problem.

No one is coming to save you. No thing, pill, other person, book, method, job, money, workshop, whatever, is going to save you. You have to save yourself.

So, in order for this method to work, you are going to have to stop making excuses or telling yourself stories and do things you don't want to do. You are going to have to take 100 percent responsibility. A good thing to keep in mind is that when you start to justify or defend your actions, that is a clear sign you don't really believe it yourself and are trying to make yourself believe it—not just others.

YOUR 85-YEAR-OLD SELF

I don't remember what book I read this exercise in, so I can't give proper credit to the author. Whoever it was, thank you. When you take the time to sit quietly and do this exercise, it is fairly powerful. Imagine yourself at eighty-five.

What would your eighty-five-year-old self tell you today? Where would your eighty-five-year-old self have wanted to live or travel, what type of work would they tell you to do now, and what would they tell you about how you should live now? Specifically, what would they tell you about what is important in your life and what is not? If you find yourself getting defensive in any way, then please pay attention to that feeling. That is your soul, your gut, telling you that you really are yearning for simplicity. The stuff doesn't matter. Especially the stuff that doesn't fit you or serve you. I have known eighty-five-year-olds. I have talked to them. Guess what? The shit doesn't matter. It never did. The shit is holding you back from what you really want.

No eighty-five-year-old has said they wished they would have worked harder or longer hours, much less that they would have bought crap they didn't need or even really want.

THE ANSWER

Okay, you have done a lot of hard work, and you are finally here and ready for the magic solution to all of your stuff problems. Here it is:

Only possess what supports or serves you and that is *you*.

It is that simple and that easy. It is a total mind shift though. It is a total gamechanger. Only have what supports or serves you, and that is you, because if you have one extra thing that doesn't, it is a burden, an anchor, a negative, and harming you.

Sounds simple enough. Here is where the work from the previous chapters comes in. Serving and supporting you means you, *not* your ego. So, if you are possessing something that is in any way tied to your ego, that means you have no business having it. It is not serving you; it is harming you.

Once you have done the work as we have, it is easier to distinguish an ego item from one that really serves or supports you. If something serves or supports you, it is an easy "hell yes!" Anything that isn't a "hell yes" is a no.

At this point, everything in my life is a "hell yes." I can easily, honestly, and articulately tell anyone how everything in my home and life serves or supports me, and why it is a "hell yes." That yoga block—I use it twice a week. That photo—I think of where I grew up and smile when I see it. Those Christmas ornaments were my grandmother's, and it makes me feel close to her when I get them out every year. They support my connection to my tribe.

If you are hesitating on an item, that is a good sign it is a no. If you didn't hesitate, it would be an instant "hell yes."

One little test that you can use to see if something is a "hell yes" item or not is to pretend. Pretend you are going to live on a tropical island or in the forest. We are pretending because your needs will be magically met, but no one else will be around. You can take anything you want, but you will need to take care of it. Again, absolutely no one will be around to see how you live. What would you take? The obvious answer is that you would only take things that are really going to support you or serve you and of course that are "you."

I have a friend whose husband, Frank, is a race car driver. Taking at least one race car to the island would be a necessity for Frank. If that man couldn't drive cars fast, on a regular basis, I don't think anyone would want to be around him. So, what may seem like a totally unnecessary item for many (a sports car) is actually serving and supporting Frank. A race car is very "Frank" and thus a necessity in his life.

So, what would you take? You certainly wouldn't take something that you have to impress others, as there is no one to impress. You aren't going to take things you don't use or don't love, as they would be a huge pain in the ass to get there as well as take care of.

The point is that this process isn't about getting rid of everything you own, only having X number of anything, or other such ridiculous ideas. It is about only having things that truly benefit your life, not your ego.

So, do you use it? That is a "hell yes." Do you love it? That is a "hell yes." Do you smile when you look at it? That is a "hell yes." Does it provide value to your life? That is a "hell yes." Is it "you"?

If impressing anyone else comes into your head when you think of it, then it is a no.

This is why you shouldn't listen to anyone about how many books you should own, how many shirts or other items of clothing you own, etc. What the hell does that person know about your life and whether something serves you or not?

If you are honest with yourself, do the hard work of self-examination, and address your ego, you really shouldn't have extras. Remember, this is a process and you will probably get rid of more and more as you go along. Depending on how much stuff you have, you might be left with very little. That can be scary, but it is incredibly liberating.

When I really got to this point, where I only had things that absolutely served me and I had no desire to keep what didn't, I had gotten rid of probably 80 percent of my property. At the beginning of this process, if someone would have told me or suggested that I get rid of 80 percent of my shit, I would have freaked out. So, NO the goal is not to get rid of X percent of your stuff. It is only to get rid of what doesn't serve or support you. That might be 10 percent of your stuff or it might be 95 percent. I don't know.

Here is what I will say. Anyone who has an exorbitant amount of stuff who tried to say it all served or supported them, I would certainly challenge. No, there isn't a magic number of things you should own, but if one is being honest with themselves, it is clear that keeping "everything" probably isn't serving you. Is keeping every picture your child has ever drawn—and your child is thirty—serving you or just keeping you stuck in the past? How is keeping more socks than you could wear in nearly a year serving you, much less old stained ones? Frank may need to take one or two race cars on his island, but thirty would probably be a bit much.

Remember, there is no neutral when it comes to the stuff. It is either a "hell yes" or a no. It is either serving you and supporting you in some way, or it is costing you, hurting you, distracting you, and serving as an anchor you don't need.

Would your life be negatively affected without it?

Another way to test whether something is a "hell yes" or not is to think how your life would be negatively affected, if at all, if you got rid of the item. The items that are "hell yes" items are those that would definitely have a negative impact if you got rid of them. For instance, if I were to get rid of my washing machine and dryer, there would be an immediate and very negative effect. I would have to spend hours each week going to a laundromat, where I probably would be uncomfortable folding my laundry in front of others, having to get quarters, and wasting time waiting for my laundry to get done, not to mention carrying laundry back and forth to the laundromat.

So, when in doubt, think about what would happen if you got rid of X. If nothing, then that is a pretty good sign you should get rid of it, as it is extra.

TIME AND COMFORT

"The only purpose of money is to provide time or comfort."

—TUCKER MAX

Here is one more way to look at whether something is serving you or not. Tucker is a friend of mine, and when he first said the above quote, I stopped and thought hard about it. I think that the same can really be said about stuff. When we are talking about our things serving us, we are really talking about whether they provide us with time or comfort.

The time is easier to understand quickly, on its surface. Will that new kitchen appliance save us time? Many promise to do so, but it is important to test their claims out to see if that appliance is actually serving us or not. For instance, take the food processor. I have one and use it when it is actually going to save me time and effort. However, in some cases, such as grating cheese, it is actually easier and takes less time for me just to grate it by hand. How, you ask? Well, by the time I get the food processor out, set up the blades, grate the cheese, and *then clean it all up* and put it away, it would have just been faster to grate it by hand and wash the hand grater or throw it in the dishwasher where it doesn't take up much space.

My point is to not just believe the party line that all of these items that are supposed to supply us with time will actually do so.

Comfort is a bit more sophisticated to think about. Physical comforts are easy to decipher. What makes us physically more comfortable generally serves us well. A comfortable mattress absolutely serves us and is worth the money. Buying an air conditioner to keep us comfortable in the summer serves us well. Having a warm coat in the winter serves us. These are all "hell yeses."

We are nearly to the point of you being able to start purging. You have worked so hard and are nearly there. I think you will actually enjoy the exercises below as they are really liberating and nourishing. Just get these done, and then you can start to purge, baby.

THE WORK

1. Are you ready to take 100 percent responsibility for making your life what you want it to be?
2. What do you know that you don't want in your life?
3. Do you know what is "you" and what is not?
4. What does your ideal life look like? What life would really nourish you, without a thought of someone else?
5. How could you get that ideal life while still being true to any real responsibilities to others?
6. What does your ideal house look and feel like? Your ideal wardrobe? Your ideal car?
7. Do you feel you are worthy of the life you want? Feel, not think. Do you feel you are worthy of a simple, easy life? Do you in any way feel a simple life would be "too easy"? What part of you craves the chaos or complexity? Why?
8. What does your eighty-five-year-old self tell you they wanted, and what is or is not important?
9. What does it mean to say that something "serves" you?
10. What will you say when your ego starts talking?

CHAPTER 7

THE ACTUAL PURGING, ONCE AND FOR ALL

"The devil is in the details, but so is salvation."

—ADMIRAL HYMAN RICKOVER

If you have done the exercises up to this point, then you have done the majority of the heavy lifting. But you are not done yet. There is still a bit more to know before you just start throwing stuff out, but we are getting there. Just starting to throw out your stuff haphazardly will result in frustration, self-defeat, and going back to trying to fill up the bottomless cup. Here are some things to keep in mind before you just start purging.

GETTING RID OF STUFF IS A PAIN IN THE ASS

Know this going in, so you have reasonable expectations. Getting rid of what doesn't serve you is totally worth it, but it is a pain in the ass. That is one of the reasons you have too much stuff to begin with. It takes time and work to get rid of the stuff. It is easier to let it sit there than to do what it takes to get rid of it. Well, that is your old mindset. If you want to change your life, you are going to have to put the time and work into doing it. I know—it sucks. Just put on your adult underwear and get to movin', as my dad used to say.

If you are like most other people, certainly most other Americans, you are going to be getting rid of a lot of shit. Just know it takes work, time, and maybe money to get rid of it. If you are really changing your mindset and life, this is NOT going to be just a few hours of tidying up on the weekend. It just isn't. It could take weeks or months to really get rid of all of your excess stuff. Yes, you do have the time and money. Do you want a simpler life or not?

TRASH

The easiest way to get rid of stuff is just to put it in the trash. However, that can still be a pain for large items. You might need to hire someone to come and take one or more things to the dump. If you can afford it, I would recommend hiring someone to come and take your large items versus trying to find a friend with a truck to help you get it to the dump.

Why? Because your time is worth a lot. Because people are busy, and it is going to take some effort and time to coordinate schedules and actually get it to the dump. All of that time, it is on your mind. The longer it takes, the less likely it is to get done. All of this time, the item is still causing harm. Just bite the bullet, pay some money, and get rid of it—now. Then it is done, and the money is well spent.

GIVE

If something is in decent shape, just give it away. Heck, put it out in front of your house with a "free" sign, and chances are it will be gone within a few hours. Problem solved. Take your bags of stuff to a charity thrift store and have it out of your life and head today. Some charity organizations will even pick up the stuff, including the big items. There is someone out there who can use that item today. If you have more sentimental, family items, see who in your family might want them. However, make sure that it is done within a week so that again, the problem is solved.

SELLING

"But I could get good money for it..."

I know many people want to sell their excess stuff. I have sold many items of mine. High-ticket items may be totally worth the time and effort to try to sell. If you have a lot of things to sell, you may want to have an old-fashioned yard sale to get rid of it in one day.

With that said, most of the time, selling stuff is a huge pain in the rear, and you get 10 percent of what you think you should get for the items, if that. If you really want to sell things, then I would suggest that you try listing it on Facebook or Craigslist for a short period of time, for half of what you think is a reasonable price, and then if it doesn't sell within one or two weeks, give it away.

I would also highly recommend avoiding consignment stores. It can take a very long time for them to sell an item, if they ever do. You are also not going to get the price you want. Yes, the item will be out of your house, but it will still be in your head. Keep getting rid of your stuff as simply as possible, and just get rid of it.

It is important that you not get hung up on wanting to make money off getting rid of your stuff. You need to be okay with just getting rid of it, even if it means giving it away. Remember, it is hurting you and the faster you can get rid of it, the better.

Clearly there are exceptions, such as high-ticket items, that will be fairly easy to sell. In that case, look on Craigslist to see what similar items are selling for, list it below that price, and it should sell quickly.

For jewelry, just take it to a used jewelry store and get what you get for it. Again, you are going to get maybe 5 to 10 percent of what you paid for it. Just accept that fact and move on.

I would also caution you about having people come to your home to pick items up. I would suggest you meet them at a public location to exchange things. If the item is large and they need to come to your house, I would have them email you a copy of their driver's license before giving them your address. Also have someone else with you. In Seattle a few years ago, a couple listed a ring on Craigslist. When the prospective buyer(s) came to pick up the ring, they shot the husband and stole the ring—in front of his wife and two small children. Be safe, as selling something is never worth jeopardizing your safety.

Also be aware of Craigslist scams. There is plenty of information online about how to avoid Craigslist scams that you can read for yourself. If something seems odd, such as someone in California wanting to buy your item in Texas, trust your gut. Accept cash only, and make the exchange in a public place if possible.

The most important thing to remember is that your first priority is to get rid of the items that are not serving you. It is not to make money. Every day that the items are in your possession is another day that you are being harmed by having too much stuff.

THE PROCESS

What is the process for starting to purge? Whatever works for you. Do that.

What works for me might not work for you. I am going to offer some suggestions below which worked for me, but honestly whatever is going to get you to start is what you need to do. Once you start the process, it should be easier and easier as your mindset is changing. This isn't about motivation, as motivation doesn't last. Motivation lasts about as long as a bath; that is why you need to take a bath every day. So, the goal isn't to get you motivated to purge. It is to change the way you think and for you to only *want* things that serve you. Your tolerance for what doesn't will be gone, and thus getting rid of it should be easy.

Just imagine the one thing in the world you have always really wanted. Doesn't matter what it is. Someone comes to you and gives you that item. You are so happy—you finally have it. Then you ask where they got it, and they answer that they found it in the Chernobyl exclusion zone. Guess what, not so attractive now is it? There is no debate in your head. You want that thing gone immediately and are a bit panicked over it.

The items that are really not serving you just came from Chernobyl—get rid of them.

For those who may not know, the Chernobyl exclusion zone

is where the Chernobyl nuclear incident occurred—everything in the zone is radioactive and will kill you.

Here are the three most important things to remember when starting to purge:

1. Get rid of the items not serving you: the "hot" radioactive items.
2. Don't get overwhelmed. How do you eat an elephant? One bite at a time. This is a huge task. It is not only physical work but also mental and emotional work. Just work on your next step, your next bite, and don't look at the huge task in front of you. Just your next bite.
3. Remember that it is a process. Don't be surprised if you do a purge, think you are done, and a few weeks later find you are ready to get rid of more stuff. It can take months or years to get down to where you really want to be, where every single thing you possess serves you. It is like stretching. At first, you can only go to a certain point, but in just even twenty or thirty seconds, your body releases and you can go another inch or two, and in another few seconds you can stretch even farther. Take your time and know that you will continue to stretch further and further—purge more and more.

Okay, so you are going to do what works for you. With that said, I am going to give you some suggestions to try, to see what works for you or what may not.

One approach is to have one day, or at least the majority of the day, dedicated to purging. That means that from X time to X time that day, you are going to do nothing but this work. Nothing but get rid of stuff. This work is going to change your flippin' life, so make it a priority. Protect that time. Do what you need to do in your life so that you have this time and it is uninterrupted. I would suggest you also do it alone. We will get to others later on. Just for now, trust me. This is your first baby step, and you want to get it done and done properly before you add other people into the mix. So, kick your family out of the house for a day. Take a day off of work—seriously. Do what you need to do.

During that one big purge, you are doing nothing else but purging. You are not checking Facebook or email, answering the phone, or cleaning your house. Remember this is hard work, so you might be tempted to get sidetracked. Don't let yourself. You are on a mission. You will be amazed by what you can get accomplished, with total focus, in six to eight hours of dedicated time. You will feel great after this purge. You will have gotten a lot accomplished and have visible results that give you instant gratification.

After your first big purge, dedicate one to two hours per week to continue the purge and calendar that time—you know if it isn't on the calendar, it doesn't get done. This keeps the momentum going without being overwhelming.

It also helps to create the habit of continually questioning if something is serving you or not.

When you are not in a dedicated time to purge, you may still notice that something catches your eye and you *know*—you *know*—it is a no. When that happens, if you are able, stop what you are doing and put that item in a designated spot or bag to purge on the next dedicated purge time. That way it isn't haunting you as much.

WHAT TO TACKLE FIRST?

This is an area where I agree with other minimalist leaders. This is a big deal, a new way of thinking, and a new way of living. You are going to want to start with easy to begin building your skills and getting some easy "wins" down first. We are going to get you walking before you try to run, much less run a marathon. If you begin with the hardest stuff first, you are likely to give up, and then you are back at square one. This is not a science. The following order is meant to start off with something easy, then move to the more difficult. If this exact order doesn't work for you, then by all means do your own thing. Do what works for you. But please start with easy and move to more difficult, not the other way around.

1. Take out the trash. This is a total give to you. This is getting a "C" in junior high gym class. There are plenty

of people out there who literally need to go through the house, pick up the trash, and take it the hell out. Even if your trash isn't completely full, just do it to give yourself a little win.

2. Old newspapers, training materials, and magazines: oh my God, you are NOT going to #$*@&@ read it. It has been sitting there for a month, six months, six years. You are NOT going to read it. Recycle it and now. You went to that workshop, seminar, or continuing education five years ago. Yes, there may be something in that notebook that at some point could help you. It isn't now, and if you need that information in the future, you can easily find it online. Really. Don't even leaf through it. That will sidetrack you. It is not serving you. GONE.

3. Kids' stuff and toys: I will address how to deal with your kids in chapter 9. For young kids, the toys and clothes that they don't use or have outgrown should be an automatic—get rid of. Do it while they aren't around in order to avoid a showdown, as the second you try to get rid of it in front of them, then they will want it. Remember, they are kids.

4. Also, if you must keep a toy from their childhood, keep one or two, not twenty—and only safe ones. For example, be careful with old toys, as they may contain lead paint. Ask me how I know about this one.

5. Old makeup and toiletries: Not only is keeping this crap hurting you in spirit, it can also actually be harming you physically. Yes, makeup companies tell you to replace

items every six months to a year because they want to sell you more stuff. AND it is because the old stuff is gross. If you took a microscope to your old mascara you wouldn't be putting it on your eyelashes anymore. So those colors that you really don't wear, that lotion that you have a reaction to, the bubble bath that you don't even really like the smell of, the travel-sized crap stuff that you took from your hotel, everything else that you are not using, that is not serving you—get rid of it. Unless you are a makeup artist, there is really no purpose in having all of that makeup. And it is gross.

6. Old cleaning products: when was the last time you actually cleaned the oven? Yet, you have two oven cleaners under the sink. You have three window cleaners, and you clean the windows once a year. Do you *really* need that special cleaner for hardwood floors? Having had hardwood floors, I can tell you, no, you don't. Again, this is an easy and fast "win." Throw them out. If they are not horrible for the sewer system, dump them out and recycle the plastic containers.

7. Other people's stuff: many of us have other people's stuff in our home, for whatever reason. Absent a very specific reason, such as your young adult child being overseas or in college for a short period of time, you have no business storing other people's things. And even your adult child...guess what? You don't need to keep their stuff. My money is on the fact that when they are *ready* to get their stuff, they won't want it. You

will have just stored that stuff for all of these years for nothing, absolutely nothing. So again, absent some rare and specific circumstances, don't let others clutter up your home and life with their crap. You are not a storage facility, and it is negatively affecting your life.

A SPECIAL NOTE ON TOILETRIES

I used to love the smell of lotions, soaps, candles, etc. The stronger the smell, the better. I also felt great when I had back-ups of soaps and lotions. Then I began, just for fun, to make my own candles, soaps, clay masks, and lotions. When one starts learning about making these items, one realizes that they are not really meant to keep for very long, other than candles, of course. If one is using natural ingredients, toiletries will not keep very long at all. They go rancid, spoil, and get moldy, depending on what one made.

You also realize that the scents don't last if they are not really strong chemicals. The more I learned, the more I went, "Ewww, I don't want that on my skin." Most candles are horrible. They are made of toxic chemicals that are only worse when they are burned. You are breathing that crap in when it is lit.

So now I only have beeswax candles that I make (or that are made by someone I trust), use essential oils for any scents, and know that smelling good is really horrible for my body due to the chemicals. So, when you really consider what you are putting on your skin or breathing, it will be far easier to immediately throw out the back supply of lotions and potions in the bathroom.

KITCHEN ITEMS

Even people who don't cook generally have a ton of crap in their kitchen. We love gadgets, tools, small appliances, and gizmos.

You use it, even if it is just once a year, or it really isn't serving you. That includes grandma's china. Use the damn china or get rid of it. Do you really think your grandma wants you to keep it in a cabinet and not use it? For what, so the next generation can keep it in a cabinet and not use it? Huh? That is ridiculous.

Also go through your pantry and get rid of whatever you thought you would use and haven't. Yes, you should have an emergency stash of food, but that doesn't need to include food that you don't even really like. That doesn't include the twenty types of vinegar you got at the farmers market. Is that product a "hell yes" and you eat that all the time? If not, give it to someone who needs to eat it today.

HOME DÉCOR, LINENS, FURNITURE, ETC.

If home décor is keeping you stuck in 1994 or you have an item to impress someone else, then get rid of it. It serves you and you love it, or it is gone. Are ten pillows on a bed really serving you? How is a wall literally covered from floor to ceiling with pictures, quotes, or whatever serving you? How is that not overstimulating?

Do you really need so many extra linens? Do you really need an extra set of sheets for the guest bedroom that someone sleeps in five times a year? How many towels do you really use each week? If you only use matching sets of linens, why are you keeping the mismatched separate items?

Furniture is another area where people have a lot more than they need. First, the easy furniture to get rid of: if it is broken or soiled, get rid of it. No, you haven't gotten it fixed or professionally cleaned thus far, and chances are you won't. Just get rid of it. It isn't serving you.

Furniture pieces are meant to work—to hold something, including you. If you have purely decorative pieces, then absent something extraordinary about them, I would ask you how are they serving you? I enjoy art as much as the next person, and furniture absolutely can be art—AND it is meant to do more than just be a piece of art. It is meant to be able to sit one's ass on or provide some other similar use.

So, go through the house and examine every single piece of furniture, element of décor, and household item. Is it a "hell yes" or not? Again, there is no question your bed is a "hell yes," as you use it every day. There is no question your dresser is a "hell yes," as it keeps your clothing clean, safe, and organized. There is no question that painting is a "hell yes," as you smile every time you look at it. If you can't immediately say "hell yes," it is a no. Any hesitation is your gut telling you it is a no.

CRAFT, HOBBIES, AND SPORTS

Even if you craft, have a hobby, or participate in a sport, keep it simple. Only have what you actually need to do the work. If you like paper arts, do you really need a small store's worth of paper? No. If you like photography, do you really need three bodies, two light meters, and six lenses? No. If you do woodworking, do you need an entire garage worth of equipment and a small forest worth of wood? No.

So, keep it simple, don't buy more than you need, and if you aren't using that tool or equipment, get rid of it.

GARAGE

The garage really gets neglected because it is just so easy to dump stuff in it and forget about it. You know that you should be able to get a car in the garage, right? You know you shouldn't be tripping over stuff in order to get to the door, right? Come on. You haven't ridden a bike in twenty years. The kids outgrew those bikes years ago. You don't do home improvement, so why do you have one, much less two, power saws? I know, I am such a jerk.

Same rules: it serves you and nurtures you in some way, or

it doesn't. There is no middle ground. **When in doubt, get it out.** This room may take some time, if you have a ton of crap in it—especially larger items that will take some effort to get rid of.

Any other category or room except for clothing and sentimental items. Now is the time to tackle any category, room, shop, or office that I haven't mentioned. Same rules: you use it, it serves you, it nurtures you in some real way, it supports you, or it's gone.

CLOTHING

What I like is to get all clothing out, so that it is visible in one place. Then only put back, into the closet or dresser, clothing that is serving you and that you feel amazing in. You don't need to feel like a movie star when you wear it, but you should feel good. Any item of clothing that you don't wear, that is uncomfortable, that makes you feel "icky" when you do wear it, or that you don't even really like doesn't go back in the drawer or closet. It isn't serving you. Those shoes that make you cry after you have worn them for an hour—or less? NOPE. They are not serving you. They literally hurt you. It doesn't matter what an item cost, who the designer is, or how cool it is. It either serves you or it doesn't.

Clothing pieces that you got on vacation because they fit

where you were vacationing, but they don't really fit where you live or your lifestyle? They need to go. They are not serving you.

A special note about clothing that you "will" fit into. Oh, I know this topic well, as I have lived it for years—okay, decades. You are a bit or a lot overweight. You have beautiful, amazing clothing that you love in your closet and you can't fit into it. *But* you will. Will you?

Are you actively behaving in ways that are likely to lead to permanent weight loss, or are you just thinking about it? If you are not actively trying to lose weight every day, then how are smaller clothes serving you? I know: to think about getting rid of them feels like you are giving up—like you just gave up the dream of ever losing weight and being able to fit into them. Somehow keeping them keeps the dream alive. But consider that if you do lose weight, are you going to even want those old clothes? Will they even be in style? Will you even want to wear them, or would you rather have some new clothes after this monumental accomplishment?

They are either serving you, it is "you," or not. Period. Pretending that they are some prize for when you lose weight isn't being honest with yourself if you are not doing the actual things that you need to do in order to lose weight. Right?

Number of Items

How many shirts or pairs of socks should you have? I don't know. And neither does anyone else. The thought of some person prescribing how many pairs of pants you should own is ridiculous. When you want to live your life by having only what serves you, you will know what is enough. Do you use fifty pairs of socks? Maybe you do. Probably not, and if not, then get rid of the ones you don't use. Continue to ask yourself how fifty pairs of socks are serving you. For the love of God, you are also not going to find the missing sock. It is gone. I don't know where they go, but it is gone. Get rid of the remaining mate.

SENTIMENTAL ITEMS AND FAMILY HEIRLOOMS

I have saved for last what is the most difficult category for most people. I have inherited a lot of items from family. At first, I felt completely obligated to keep everything. I felt like even thinking about not wanting it was not respectful to my relative, not loving them, or not honoring them some-how—even completely disrespecting my entire heritage. Or I worried that I would somehow forget about them without their stuff everywhere to remind me of them. If I got rid of my son's baby clothes or drawings he made as a kid, I was a horrible mother—even though the items had been stored away for decades.

Much of the stuff wasn't even special to me. I didn't have

any memory connected to it other than it had been my aunt's, mom's, cousin's, or even a neighbor's. Some of the stuff was beautiful. Some I used. Most of it I didn't.

Over the years, I was able to slowly begin to get rid of the family stuff. In some cases, I gave things to other family members who wanted the item. In many other cases, I just gave the items away.

One day, I tackled my mom's and aunt's papers—old letters, yearbooks, and pictures. They were from high school and college. I didn't know the people who wrote the letters, nor did they mean anything to me. They were a part of my aunt's and mom's history, not mine. We are all going to die, friend. We are all going to go into history. My aunt died when I was eight. Why did I need her college diploma? Yes, she had worked hard to get it, and I was proud of her for doing so. Her education and career legacy for me is that she taught me to read and to love to read. That is her legacy, not an old diploma for me to carry around until I die and then dump on someone else.

Like me, this is an area where many people struggle with getting rid of stuff that isn't serving them. If that is you, may I suggest: if your relative were able to talk to you, I am quite certain they would not want you to be burdened with their old stuff.

You are under no obligation to keep old photos, furniture, papers, or anything else of someone else's that isn't serving or supporting you—*even* family heirlooms. Once you really know if something is serving you or not it, it will be far easier to let go of things. You know it is a burden on you, haunting you every time you walk by the crystal set that you haven't used, ever.

If you absolutely can't part with whatever, then by God, start using it. No, the earth will not open up and swallow you if you use the good china for pizza tonight. Even if something breaks, it is okay. The items are meant to be used. What in the world is the purpose of having them if you are not going to use them?

That is really about it. I don't feel any less close to my family. Their memory is still very fresh in my mind, and other people are enjoying the items that I wasn't using. What better way to honor them would there be?

GET IT GONE

This may sound ridiculously elementary—and yes, I am repeating myself a bit—but once you have designated an item as gone, then immediately, or as soon as humanly possible, get rid of it! Time is of the essence. So, reserve an hour at the end of purging days to deliver the stuff to the donation site or dump. Make arrangements for the pickup of larger items—that very same day if possible. Get the trash out to the curb, even if trash day is a few days away. If mailing sentimental items to relatives, then get your rear to the post office and get it done.

Why such urgency? It is all psychological, friend. The faster it is out of your control, the sooner your brain doesn't register it as "yours" anymore. Especially at the beginning, when your skills of deciding whether or not something really serves you are not fully developed, your ego may start trying to talk you into keeping X. If it is gone, even on the curb, your brain isn't thinking about it much.

There is a big difference between "I am going to let it go" versus "I have let it go." You want the stuff out of your house, life, and head. The sooner it is in someone else's hands, the better.

WHAT ABOUT OTHER PEOPLE IN YOUR HOUSE?

I talk much more about dealing with other people in the next chapter. However, just to touch on how to actually purge with others living in your house, I will briefly say the following. If you live with people who are on the same team and want a simpler life, then great, you can work together. Just remember to concentrate on your own stuff and not theirs. Also, their timing may be different from yours. Stay in your own lane.

For those in homes in which other people don't share your newfound excitement to get rid of stuff, don't worry about them. For right now, just purge your own shit. Don't even think about your spouse's crap from high school or your kids' stuff. Just work on your own stuff.

You have every right to get rid of your own stuff. You don't even need to tell them what you are doing—just do it.

THE BIG KAHUNA: YOUR HOUSE

This section was such a touchy subject with me that I literally procrastinated writing about it until I was nearly ready to send my first draft to my editor. Unlike any other property, your home can be very touchy and painful. If you are getting any resistance to even reading this section, then pay attention to that. That resistance may be trying to protect you from the ugly truth. If there weren't a problem with your house, you wouldn't feel the need to protect or defend it. Yes, it is fine to flip me off right about now. I am not suggesting taking any action—really. I am just suggesting that you think about whether your home is actually serving you or if you are serving your home.

As I have already written, I have loved houses since I was a child. I have owned my own home since I was thirty years old, and even then I felt late to the party. Owning your own home is the American dream and is seen as the fastest and safest way to build wealth. It is an immense source of pride—or so we are told, over and over again.

All of those things can be true, if your home is serving you. But let me tell you...if you are serving your house, your life can be an absolute nightmare. Ask anyone who has lost their home in a foreclosure. They will probably still tear up when talking about the stress, shame, embarrassment, and feeling of failure.

Ask someone about a major remodel of their house, much less a total renovation of an old home. Your dream can very quickly turn into a total nightmare.

It is easy to lie to ourselves and justify keeping a home that isn't serving us. We have a lot of ego tied into our home. Let me be clear. I am not suggesting everyone sell their home and move into a smaller home. I am suggesting, strongly, that you *honestly* examine whether your home is serving you, or the other way around. If your home is continually causing financial stress—if you are house poor—that is a problem. And no, I am not talking about a short-term financial stress because you are fixing it up. I am talking about continually being financially stressed over this home.

If your home takes so much upkeep, cleaning, and maintenance that it is causing you stress, you aren't able to keep up with it, or you are even resentful about the amount of work, then maybe it is too much. Even if you have people helping you, is it still a pain in the ass? Is your house just so damn big that it isn't comfortable, or you only go into that room once or twice a year? Do you feel any resentment toward your house? Are you living in your home to show your wealth? Is your home even you? Do you feel your absolute most comfortable in your home?

Those are all things you should pay attention to. It may take some time, but if your house isn't serving you, why are you still living in it? What would your life be like in another home that did serve you? Imagine a home that you could easily afford, without any financial stress—or a home that was beautiful and had everything you wanted, but didn't require all the upkeep of your current home. Again, go back to what the heck you really want in life. This is where you go to sleep every night and wake up every morning. It should absolutely be you.

You might also consider what a smaller home might be able to do for your family. I knew a lady, Micki, who was married with three children. She and her husband had plenty of money and owned a large home on an island outside of Seattle. The home was a lot of work, and she noticed that the family was not spending as much time together as a unit as she wanted. The kids all went to their separate rooms, shut the door, and did their own thing. Micki and her husband started to simplify their lives and knew their house was too big for them. So, they sold it and moved into a friend's cabin. This cabin was less than 1,000 square feet, and the kids shared a bedroom. It was on an amazing piece of property with lots of trees and a swimming area into the Puget Sound.

When hearing this story, the first thing that comes into many people's heads is "Oh, I bet the kids fought a lot in such close quarters." Nope—quite the opposite, given the extremely limited space the family had to be together. There wasn't room not to be. The kids started playing together more, helping each other with homework, and wanting to be together as a family. They started climbing trees to read books. I swear it was like reading a passage from *Anne of Green Gables* or some other romantic childhood novel. But it was all true. They had the best time as a family.

A few years in, Micki and her family bought another home that was a bit larger than the cabin, but they would never go back to the large family home they had before, ever again, regardless of their income, maintenance, or any other factor. A smaller home was just better for them and more conducive to their family unit spending time together.

The important thing is to not have tunnel vision and think that you *have* to have a home of X size. Maybe that size will serve you and maybe not. Be open to the possibilities.

Back to the basics. Does your home serve you? All of you. Is it "you"? Hell yes, or is it a no? If it is a no, then it is time to either make your home more you or start the process of getting into a home that is you.

So, let's get to work on getting rid of anything that isn't serving you or isn't really you. Take your time to do this work, and remember it is a process and you will be able to do more and more over time.

THE WORK

1. What is your plan to begin the purging process?
2. How will you set aside time and eliminate distractions in order to keep you on track and focused?
3. How will you dispose of big items?
4. Is your first major purge day calendared?
5. Are your minor subsequent purging times calendared?
6. Are you clear on knowing if something serves you or not?
7. After your major purging day, please take some time and journal about how you feel. How did it feel to get rid of items that didn't serve you? What other thoughts or feelings came up? No judgment, just write it all down. Keep doing this throughout your purging process. Did any resistance or fear surface? How did you address it?
8. Is your home serving you?
9. Is your business serving you?

CHAPTER 8

MOVING FORWARD

Alright, you have taken the time and energy to purge. You should feel so proud of yourself. Your home, office, workspace, whatever, should be far less cluttered, your brain feels better, and life is good. How do you make sure that you never go back there?

First, remember that this isn't just a new way to simplify or organize your stuff. This is a new way of life. This is a new way in which you want to live—a way that will change everything. It isn't about organizing the stuff. It is about your life.

ARE YOU WORTHY?

At the risk of getting into what some would call "woo-woo" shit, I am going to ask you to think about whether you really feel worthy of living in a clean, tidy, organized, and peaceful space. People only get what they think they are worthy of receiving. I can tell you, yes, you are worthy, even if you don't fully believe it. You are worthy of having a clean and tidy place to live.

HELL YES, OR IT IS A NO

You have this new life. Does that mean you are never going to buy something ever again? No. You are going to need more clothing or whatever in the future. First, be aware of your weak spot, whether it is clothing, home goods, tools, or whatever. If you know you are going into a situation where your defenses may be tested, then armor up by reminding yourself of the new life-guiding principle of "It is an instant hell yes, or it is a no."

Regardless of the situation, the rules of your new life still apply. You either want this new life or you don't. So, when faced with buying anything, the answer to whether you get it or not is the same. It is either a "hell yes," or it is a no. No exceptions. No excuses. No stories. And again, if there is any hesitation, that means your gut is trying to tell you it is a "no."

This is the absolute most important principle to keeping your life simple and free of excess stuff. Be honest with yourself. When you start to talk yourself into an item, stop and walk away. Only buy it from your heart, not your head.

Remember, it doesn't matter how great an item is if it isn't "you."

HOW TO STAY THE COURSE

"Hell yes, or it is a no" is your guiding principle for every decision. However, there are plenty of other helpful tools to use in order to keep you firm in your new life.

KEEP YOUR EGO IN CHECK

With all of the work you have done, you may have put a temporary muzzle on your ego, but it is still very much there. Be aware of it, and work on being able to tell when it is your ego talking, not your gut—when you want to buy something to impress others, to "feel good," because you "deserve it," or whatever. You know yourself. Just be aware of who is actually talking in your head. If it is your ego, shut it down—and fast.

RENT OR BORROW–DON'T BUY

You can rent so many things in today's world, even clothing. If you need to wear a fancy outfit, how about renting it instead of buying it? Borrow your friend's lovely diamond earrings for that special night out. You don't need to buy your own. Don't ever be embarrassed to ask to borrow something that you don't use on a regular basis.

If you need that tool, rent it. You may *need* that tool once every five years. Why buy it? Just rent it. Generally, it is really easy and cheap. Then you don't have the burden of having it lying around year after year.

Even with large purchases, rent before you buy. If you think you want to live in a cabin in the woods, then go rent one for six months to see if you really love it or not. Had I implemented this hack, it would have saved me from buying a small, nonworking farm in the middle of Texas.

Think you love that new fancy car? Rent it for a month and see if the "shiny ball" syndrome has gone away. Many times, we just need to scratch that itch. We don't really want or need X forever; we just want that feeling for a bit. So, go get that itch scratched without the time, energy, money, and hassle of owning it.

For me, I absolutely want the experience of living in different places around the world and living in different homes. I want to live in a very modern home, a cabin in the Swiss Alps, a flat in Paris and Istanbul. That doesn't mean I need to own any of these homes. I just need to scratch the itch. So maybe I live in Paris for a year and the other places for four to six months. That is all I need. Especially with the advent of Airbnb, it has never been easier to rent a fabulous home anywhere in the world.

ONE IN, ONE OUT

Another principle to keep in mind is for every item you bring into your life, another one should be removed. This doesn't need to apply to consumable products such as food, toiletries, etc. So, if you buy a shirt, then take another item of clothing you don't like as much out of the mix and donate it. Don't get hung up and think it needs to be the same or a similar item, but don't cheat by bringing in an item and then getting rid of a paperclip as your one out. If you find yourself even thinking of cheating, you should question your motives and what is really going on emotionally. No shame, just get in touch with the feelings.

Obviously, this also doesn't apply if you actually need the item. For instance, at one point I was down to only a few T-shirts. I wear them all of the time, and many had simply worn out. So, the next time I traveled, I picked up a few from places that meant a lot to me to replace the ones I had already disposed of in the last year or so.

Don't overthink this or get too rigid about it. The point is that you are continually keeping the level of your stuff at a relative status quo—after you are down to only "hell yes" items.

COUNT TO TEN–OR ONE HUNDRED
The more you live this lifestyle, the weaker the temptation

will be to buy excess, or anything that is not a "hell yes." But you are still human, and your ego is never going to disappear. So, when you see something and your excitement builds and your eyes start getting wide, take ten. Chill the hell out, take a walk, and come back the next day. There isn't anything wrong with you. You haven't failed; this is just a test. Go back to your basics and how you want to live.

Recently this happened to me. Imagine writing a book on not being attached to stuff and then having that "ohhhh-hhhhhhhhhh" feeling at the thought of buying stuff that really wouldn't serve me. I needed new sunglasses. My old frames were outdated, and my hair had always caught on one part of the sunglasses. I also wanted a second pair of regular glasses in case something happened to my primary pair, as I am blind without them. Would having a few sets of glasses serve me? Absolutely. So, I just googled "fun eyeglass frames" and found a website with the most spectacular and fun frames—all different colors and shapes, and I could afford them. Holy shit, I was in trouble. I immediately felt the excitement. My heart rate sped up a bit and I was thinking, *Wow, I could get like ten pairs and have so much fun with them.* I swear it was like I was five and had just walked into a candy store with no adult supervision.

Thankfully, within a few seconds, I caught myself and literally got up from the computer and walked out of the room to get a cup of tea. Two frames would serve me well, and I could afford them. More importantly, I know myself, and I wouldn't wear the other seven or eight pairs. I might for the first week, and then the novelty would wear off and they would sit in a drawer. Then at some point, after feeling guilty for getting them in the first place, or getting them and not wearing them, I would come to my senses and decide to get rid of them. Then someone else would have to replace the lenses, as they are prescription glasses.

Within twenty seconds, I had managed to center myself again and was able to calmly look at the website, pick one I would wear on a daily basis, and feel good about buying them.

So, when you see or hear of something and get "that feeling"—you know the one I am talking about—of excitement and glee, reminiscent of how a child acts in a candy or toy store, slow the hell down. Literally go take a walk, count to ten or one hundred if you need to, and get centered again. *Do not* make any purchase while you are in that mindset. You will absolutely regret it almost the minute you do.

Also take a few minutes to examine what just happened and why—again, not in your head, but in your heart. What triggered you, and why now? Are you having a bad day or feeling deprived in some way, or what else gave your ego fuel to get crazy like that? Just take note and congratulate yourself for catching yourself. That is a big deal.

TRAVELING

Buying items when you travel can be a more difficult subject, so I am devoting a small section to just that. I trust that at this point, you are over any desire to buy nonsense souvenir crap that no one needs or wants. But most people do want to bring home a few treasures from their travels. In my past, I have gone crazy with buying things when I travel, to the point of having to ship a huge box home from London once.

My first big trip after my simplifying my life, I have to admit I was a bit nervous. I was going to Ireland and began to calmly prepare for what I might want to buy. That way, temptation wouldn't get the better of me in the heat of the moment. I reminded myself that I was going for the experience, not the stuff. I really had no desire for crystal, whereas before, I would have come home with five or six pieces. I lived in Texas, so a big thick wool sweater was ridiculous, and I limited my gifts for others. As it turned out, I only got a few gifts for people, things they would actually use, and a few items I would actually use regularly.

I left Ireland with only my carry-on suitcase and my handbag. It felt amazing. I have great treasures from my trip, but not too much. Everything was a "hell yes." I remember easily walking through the airport and looking at items in the shops that I normally would have wanted to purchase. Not only was I not even tempted, now I just saw what a burden trying to get those items home would be without breaking some of them. I felt so free, easily walking through the airports without carrying a bunch of stuff. I was even more relaxed on the long flight home.

I also experienced an unexpected benefit from not buying many things on this trip. Normally, I would have planned out which shops I wanted to go to and things I wanted to take home with me. I had none of that on this trip. It was a completely different experience. I had far more time to just walk around and explore the city. I had no anxiety about having to find a shop or item. I had no temptation to buy things, even lovely things, when I did go into shops. I sat in a park for hours, just enjoying the park and watching people. I sat in a library and just read. I spent my time in a local pub, chatted with other customers, and just soaked up the atmosphere. I felt like I absorbed the experience, instead of just witnessing it.

EXPERIENCES, NOT STUFF

We are not here to collect stuff. We have many different purposes, but one of them is to have experiences. Always place the value, and put the money, into experiences and not stuff. So, when the choice is taking that trip or buying X, then take the trip. That is where the memories come from, the bonding with family takes place, where your life changes—not with the stuff.

So, take the class, travel, go out to dinner with friends, do the thing you are scared to do...but take the experience over the stuff. What experience are you missing out on when you are in the store shopping for stuff you don't need or really want? Remember that. You could be taking a walk in the forest or on the beach. You could be getting a massage or having lunch with an old friend.

You are here for the experience, not the stuff.

GIFTS

Giving to others—I used to love giving gifts. I spent a lot of time and energy picking out just the perfect gift. Even when I couldn't afford it, I bought people good gifts and overgifted.

Now, my gifting habits are extremely different. I still enjoy giving gifts. But now I am extremely thoughtful about what I am giving and why. I have a few people in my life who are really struggling financially. I try to give them items that they can actually use and that will make a direct impact on their day. I also give them cash. For everyone else, they don't *need* a damn thing. So, I give experiences, consumables, or something totally unique that I know they will use.

Some years ago, I gave my teenage cousin, Tom, cash for Christmas with some suggestions. Tom could use the cash for whatever he wanted...or we could use an amount he chooses and go and give it to someone in need. He got to decide. Tom is a great kid, and I knew what he would do. He took the vast majority of the money, and we went out for the day. He wanted to give it to one homeless man in particular, but we couldn't find him. So, we went to a mission in downtown Seattle. This was an eye-opening experience for both Tom and me, as neither of us had ever been in a homeless shelter. What we heard and saw that day still brings a tear to my eye, even years later. Tom gave the attendant at the shelter nearly his entire Christmas gift. While we were there, some people came in looking for a place to sleep that night and were told the shelter was full. After we left, Tom asked me where those people were going to sleep that night. I told him I didn't know.

Yes, Tom did keep a bit of the money and enjoyed getting himself some music. And the impact that that gift had on him and his life were far greater than if I had given him one hundred times the amount in the form of any other sort of gift.

So, when you are giving a gift, think about whether the person will love it and use it, or whether it is actually going to be a burden to them (whether they know it or not). Also give them permission to get rid of it if they don't really want it.

RECEIVING GIFTS

Just because you have completely changed your view on stuff doesn't mean other people have. Well-meaning people will give you gifts that are far from "hell yeses," and you will need to deal with that gracefully. The more you purge and have a simpler life, the more people will be conscious of what they give to you—hopefully. I think it is also perfectly fine to tell people who regularly give gifts to you that if they give you gifts in the future, you would prefer consumable items or whatever. If someone continues to buy you things after you have indicated you would prefer not to have things, then pay attention. First know that it has nothing to do with you, but with them. Gifting can, frankly, be a manipulation tool. You are perfectly free to establish boundaries regarding receiving gifts from people. You are not obligated to take things you don't want.

Obviously, show gratitude for the thought and gesture. Whether you say anything about keeping the gift is up to you and the situation.

SIX-MONTH REVIEWS

Every six months or so, I do a quick review of my house to see what I have accumulated that I no longer want, or what else isn't serving me. What else am I ready to let go of? At the beginning, you may continually find items that you are okay with letting go of now. As time moves on, that will likely lessen and you might come to a time when you find there is nothing else to let go of. It is a process, like taking layers off of a piece of baklava—one thin layer at a time. So again, don't be surprised if you think you are done, only to find yourself getting rid of more stuff in six months, a year, and a few years later. It is all part of the process. The process gets easier over time, the more you live a simpler life.

AM I FIXED NOW?

First of all, you were not broken. But the answer is no. Even if you have successfully been able to get rid of your extra belongings and feel amazing, you will always need to watch for any fallbacks. The goal is not to punish yourself for ever having something that doesn't serve you. The goal is to be conscious and catch yourself quickly if you ever start to slip. It will become easier and easier over time, until you really don't want anything and the thought of it gives you an instant uneasy feeling.

Do not underestimate your ego. It is still there and will be waiting for you. You don't need to be militant, but you do need to be conscious and never get lulled into thinking that you have this thing totally licked. That is when it will bite you.

THE GREEN-EYED MONSTER–JEALOUSY

You are on the right track, have purged a lot of stuff, and feel great. You love this new life of yours. And then you go to a friend's house that is big, and beautiful and has lovely, shiny things. And you start to "go there." *Oh, this home is lovely and look at all of her nice things and that car.* It is so easy to go there, especially when you are out of your physical environment. Just don't go there. In your head, picture a stop sign. STOP. Remember why you are doing this. Think about the true cost of all the pretty things. And do you really think your friend is happier than you?

I know it can be difficult, especially if you have a bad day. I have some very wealthy friends. When I spend time in their homes and around their stuff, I can, for a few seconds, feel the green-eyed monster coming into my head. That is my ego, and I have to tell it to stop. My friends' homes, stuff, and life would not fit me. I am creating the life that I want and that serves me. I can have anything I want, as long as it serves me.

THE WORK

1. What is your plan to deal with any feelings of want which may come up in the future?
2. What are your triggers? How will you prepare for them? How will you deal with them when you are triggered?
3. Do you feel fairly secure moving forward? If not, why

not? What is your fear? How are you addressing that fear?

4. If you do acquire things in the future that don't serve you, what is your plan to deal with that situation?

{ CHAPTER 9 }

THE FALLOUT

"Ignore those that make you fearful and sad, that degrade you back towards disease and death."

—RUMI

Why in the hell would anyone else care if you get rid of your shit? Why did people give me crap about not liking salmon? The answers are complex, but make no mistake: many people will freak the hell out when you begin to simplify your life. There are consequences to this massive shift in one's life, and there will be fallout. People won't understand, will feel threatened, and will feel judged, and it can be difficult. Of course, none of that makes sense logically, but again, we aren't talking about logic, are we? It is all about the feelings.

The fallout can be managed if you know what is coming.

And getting the life you want is totally worth any pushback from other people.

DEALING WITH OTHERS

Before anything else, please sear it into your mind that your stuff is your stuff to do with as you wish. It is no one else's business what you do with it. Really.

Most people who learn that you are downsizing (simplifying, purging, whatever you want to call it) will make a comment similar to "Oh, that is great—I need to do that." They are probably thinking along the lines of "organizing" the garage and taking a load of stuff to the thrift shop. They are not thinking a total change in mindset about stuff and an entirely new lifestyle.

Whenever you improve your life, it can be threatening to other people. They love you and want the best for you, but when you make a major shift in your life, it creates a mirror in which their own crap is reflected back to them, and that can be very uncomfortable. So instead of dealing with their own insecurities, ego issues, and issues with stuff, they find fault with what you are doing. "This" is too extreme. "What if you need that someday?" "I can't believe you are getting rid of that." "I don't know why you get rid of stuff; you are only going to buy it back." "I can't believe you are getting rid of your grandmother's stuff." These are just a few of the comments I have heard from people in my life when I have gotten rid of stuff.

People are people and, just like crabs, when one starts to climb out of the bucket, the others try to grab it and pull it back in. When you decide to take your health seriously and start to eat vegetables, what do people around you do? Do they instantly start eating vegetables, too? No, they continue to eat the crap and either make excuses for it or taunt you with it. Some even try to sabotage you. "Oh, just eat one cupcake, it isn't going to kill you." It is a defense mechanism. Same goes with this healthy change in lifestyle. Other people are not automatically going to get on board.

It still may throw you a bit, but know it is their crap—not yours.

Every time you get rid of a book, they are reminded that they really have too many or are way too attached to them. Every time you take another carload of stuff to the thrift store, they are reminded that they, too, have clothing in their closet that they will never wear yet can't seem to part with. No one wants to admit that their identity or self-worth is attached to possessions.

Remember, they have bought into the BS commercialism as well. Just because you have now started to see how ridiculous having all the stuff is, doesn't mean they have. They still believe that stuff = happiness, success, respect...whatever. You are the person shouting that the emperor has no clothes, and that is threatening to them, as they will have to admit they bought into the BS. Don't judge them. They are just at a different spot than you are. Just go about your business and do what you need to do for your life.

It has taken me a while, but if someone isn't in the ring with me, battling the same battles I am battling, I am really not interested in their feedback. If you have never faced the issue I am facing, I am not interested in your feedback. What lifestyle you choose for yourself and your family, and how much stuff you have, is really no one else's business. Really. You are doing what is right for you. "I am not interested in your feedback" is fine to think and to say out loud.

Establishing healthy boundaries with people is a good and necessary thing. So, when someone makes rude, harmful, or inappropriate comments, it is fine to establish a boundary by telling them anything you are comfortable saying such as...

- "Thank you for your concern, and this is what I am doing."
- "I'm really not interested in your feedback."
- "I'm an adult, and I get to choose what I have or don't have."

OTHERS IN YOUR HOME

Always keep in mind that this is your journey, not theirs. That may sound a bit harsh, but it is true. Remember your purpose. Getting rid of what doesn't serve you will make room for what does and will improve your life in ways you don't even know are possible. This might sound too good to be true, but once you taste the freedom of not being attached to what doesn't serve you, then you begin to look at what else may not serve you in your life. You begin to create a life that you love and that fits you. So don't let anyone else and their emotional baggage deter you.

For now, just concentrate on your own stuff. The surest way to derail this process in a home is to start pointing the finger at the other people in your home. You can't force this way of thinking on other people. You can show them the watering hole, but you can't make them drink—and trying to force them, guilt them, or otherwise manipulate them will backfire.

With that said, it is perfectly acceptable to calmly explain the impact of living in a home with too much stuff. In fact, I encourage you to do so. I once had a client, Bill, who had fought with his wife about the state of their home for many years. While I was working with them, he nearly broke down and explained to her how it felt to live in such chaos, how it affected his anxiety, and his feelings toward their life together. His wife got it and was able to make changes. She loved him, and his emotional well-being was more important to her than the stuff. That shift only happened when he calmly and vulnerably explained his feelings to her.

Don't attack them, but do calmly explain how their keeping these items makes you feel, how having all of this clutter makes your anxiety go up, and how you don't feel valued when they continue to buy X, Y, and Z, when the household can't afford it. Explain specifically how their stuff is negatively affecting your life.

Except when dealing with a small child, don't get rid of other people's stuff without their explicit permission—even your spouse's crap that has been stored in the basement for a decade. It is not yours to get rid of, and it will cause a lot of turmoil and resentment if you get rid of their stuff. Believe me—I know from personal experience.

A special note about stuff from past relationships. Get rid of it. You are either out of the relationship or not. No one entering a relationship with you wants to see your old pictures of your ex-wife, sit in "her" chair, or feel like they are living in your ex-husband's home. It is weird and disrespectful to anyone entering your life. I once knew a woman, Carol, who was married with two small children. Her mother-in-law had clearly wanted her son to marry his ex-girlfriend, and she kept their picture up in her home. Her grandchildren would ask why the woman was in the picture with Daddy. How screwed up is that? It was beyond disrespectful to Carol, her marriage, and her children.

Even if your spouse passed away and you want to keep a few things of his or hers, keep a few things, not the entire house. How do you think your new spouse feels walking into *her* home when it looks and feels like your first spouse's?

When you make a fresh start from a relationship, then make a fresh start. At least change the freakin' sheets, people. Get new stuff or at least paint the old. No one wants to feel like they are entering your life and competing with your ex or living in his or her world.

If your spouse or significant other choses the stuff over your well-being, then that is probably something you should pay attention to. Any time you live with other people, you are going to have to compromise. However, you shouldn't have to live in a home that is negatively affecting your life or making you feel like crap. That is not okay.

Regardless of your situation, hopefully the other people in your home will see what you are doing, see what a difference it is making in your life, and want a bit of that feeling for themselves. You are going to be far more influential just by changing your own life for the better rather than trying to preach, manipulate, or force others to get rid of their stuff. Just focus on your own stuff, and don't worry about theirs.

CHILDREN

Depending on the age of your children, you can really prevent or undo some of the damage of being attached to your stuff. Talk to your kids about what you are doing and why. Kids are much smarter and more intuitive than we give them credit for. They really don't want all of the stuff. They don't want to be overwhelmed or live in a chaotic environment.

You might be surprised by just how easy it is to get kids to voluntarily give up their extra stuff when it is just part of the routine. If you can teach this habit to your kids, you will be giving them such an incredible gift. You may want to use other language that they will understand a bit more than the word "service" and "support," such as this item "helps us." Or you can limit the number of items that they can have at any one time, and then let them choose what they have. So say, for instance, "In our house we have five dolls" or something similar, and then let them pick out their favorites and let the others go to other nice homes. Absent them being fairly young, don't just go into their room and remove their stuff, though, as that can be fairly dramatic and traumatizing. How would you like it?

Here is what I would do with children if I could do it over again. First, remember that children don't listen to what we say but do as we do. They can also smell a hypocrite from a mile away. So, there is no way you are going to get them on board until they see you getting rid of your own stuff. Also, remember the goal of getting rid of their stuff is secondary to teaching them not to have their stuff attached to their ego and to not wanting too much stuff in the first place.

Once they see you purging, they are going to want to join in, or at least their curiosity will be piqued. Then, do it together and make it a regular part of your life. Make it fun, not a chore. Absolutely no yelling, getting frustrated, putting unreasonable timeframes on it, etc. If you do it poorly, you will be making it a traumatic event and instilling the exact opposite of what you want.

If your kids are teens, well, good luck to you. Remember, they are pushing away from you for a reason, and that is a healthy thing. Depending on the teen, I think the most you can do is set a good example and maybe, softly, quietly, try to tell them about what you are doing and hope they pick some of it up. The more you push them to get rid of their stuff, the more they will refuse to do so, and again, you will be instilling the opposite habits that you want them to have.

One last note on children: they are their own individuals and not just an extension of you. Whether they as adults are tidy, attached to stuff, etc., may or may not be due to their childhood, but it is not a report card on you as a parent. My children have always lived in clean and tidy homes. I will also talk about my biological son Jonathan and not my stepsons, as Jonathan never split his time living in my home with anyone else. Since Jonathan and I have lived on our own, when I was nineteen and he was five, he has lived in a tidy, clean, and clutter-free home. Jonathan does not share my thoughts or feelings on keeping his living space clean and tidy. Jonathan is a full-grown adult and can live in any environment he sees fit. It is none of my business. It is not a reflection of the way in which I raised him. It is none of my business. It is none of my business. It is none of my business. Are you getting the point?

FILLING THE VOID

I know this is going to sound ridiculous, but stay with me. When you radically simplify your life, you are going to have extra money and a lot of extra time—so much time you may even get bored. Sounds amazing, right? I thoroughly believe in the benefits of boredom. This is where the creative ideas flow, the thoughts that one needs to deal with are free to come up, and the mind can rest. However, just like everything else, too much boredom can turn into a negative space quickly.

If you do not fill this time with something purposeful, then other things will fill it—probably not things you want to have your time filled with. You have come too far to live purposefully to spend hours each day on Facebook; Netflix binges; saying yes to volunteer opportunities that you don't really want to do, but you feel guilty saying no as you have the time; or heaven forbid, starting to window shop either in person or online, just because you are bored.

So, before you get to that place, start to think of other things you would rather be doing with your free time. At this point, it may be hard to imagine that you will have free time, but trust me, you will. Do you want to read more? Learn to play the piano? Give to others in the way you want to give? Take that painting class just for fun? Start exercising again? You could spend more one-on-one time with your kids, without phones. Be as specific as possible, since "exercising" doesn't mean the same as "take four exercise classes each week" or "hike two times per week."

The point is that you are purposefully filling your time each day with things that will nourish you, support you, and bring you joy. Someone else is not filling your day with the things they want you to do. This is regardless of how much free time you have. Of course, we all have responsibilities to others and ourselves that may not bring us a tremendous amount of joy. However, the more purposeful you are about how you spend all of your time, not just your free time, the more satisfying life will be.

The same goes for money. I hope, now that you are no longer spending money on things you don't really love and don't serve you, that you will have a cushion every month to spend as you really want to spend—whether that is to have a savings cushion, pay off debt, take amazing trips, or give to others. Maybe you will even have enough to be able to quit that job you hate and do something you really want to do. Again, I would suggest you begin to at least think about how you would like to use the money you are no longer spending on stuff.

If you are not purposeful about it, the money and time will likely disappear.

THE WORK

1. Who in your life is going to have a difficult time with you simplifying your life and getting rid of excess stuff?
2. Are you able to identify why they might have issues with it? Are you able to clearly see that those issues are their issues?
3. Is your stuff any of their business?
4. What is your plan to deal with that resistance from others?
5. What will you say to respectfully set a firm boundary?
6. What are you going to do with your extra time?
7. What are you going to do with your extra money?

CHAPTER 10

FREEDOM, THE REAL PRIZE

"The secret of happiness is freedom, and the secret of freedom is courage."

—THUCYDIDES

The real gift that comes with such simplicity is freedom. The freedom to live how you want to live. The freedom to do what you want to do and only have what works for you. The freedom to quit that job that you hate. The freedom to move to where you wish to live. The freedom to write that book you have always wanted to write or learn how to play the piano. The freedom to be you. The freedom to define what "success" means to you and to live accordingly.

But that freedom is not free. You will be paying a price for that freedom, as you will be rejecting what most others in this culture value. The price is completely worth it.

Make no mistake about it: really simplifying your life, especially your relationship with stuff, is not a trivial matter. It is a complete change in mindset, a change in your values, and a change of your life. The real prize in owning only what serves you is freedom and total comfort—about as much freedom as a person can ever have. Freedom from want. Freedom from financial burdens. Physical freedom. Freedom to pursue your purpose. Freedom from giving a shit what others think, or at least doing so less than before.

It is having everything you own totally fit you in every possible way.

Until you get to the other side of wanting stuff and not being attached to it, you really don't realize just how heavy a burden you have been carrying. Just how much your self-esteem was tied to what you own. Just how much time and energy you spend caring for your stuff, worrying about your stuff, or even just thinking about it. How much of your life did you trade making money to buy the stuff? How much pressure did you put on yourself to make that money in order to buy the stuff?

You may still enjoy the remaining things you have, but you are not attached to them. You know in your head, but especially your heart, that if you lost everything, you would still be okay. You as a person would remain exactly as you are. You are not your things. They are not a reflection of who you are as a person or your worth. You as a person are not in any way dependent on what you possess. That is freedom, friend.

When you begin to look at your possessions as simply props in a play that are only there to serve you, everything changes and frees up.

What happens when you begin to really get rid of your attachment to stuff is that your values change. Your idea of success changes. We have been told for centuries what it means to be successful. And most certainly in today's age, there is no doubt as to the pressure to conform to what we as a society say is "success." When you define "success" for yourself instead of accepting what others think "success" is, you get the most incredible feeling of freedom. You feel freedom in your bones, friend.

When you begin to really let go of your attachments to stuff, your values start to change. You begin to look at money differently. It is not something to be acquired in order to keep score, try to get self-esteem, or to buy crap. It is something to earn in order to allow you to live the life you truly want to live.

You no longer have a desire to work fifty, sixty, or eighty

hours a week, much less at a job you hate, in order to buy more stuff. You want to spend more time with your family. You want to spend more time with yourself, doing things you actually enjoy. Not feeling the need to overwork is freedom.

Success no longer means how much money you make that year, what your net worth is, how much is in your portfolio, or what sort of countertops you have in your kitchen. Your idea of success pivots to whether you are doing what you love to do every day. How much of an impact you are making in the world for other people. Whether the people who are supposed to love you actually, in fact, love you. Whether you are happy every day.

Make no mistake: this shift doesn't mean you shouldn't have wealth, amazing clothes, and marble countertops. There is nothing wrong with having nice things or money. It is a very fine line, and it takes some work to walk it without falling into the abyss of materialism and consumerism. Again, it goes back to your why. Do you have that $1,000 coat because you love it, it is "you," and it is such a quality piece that you will wear it for twenty years? Or do you have that $1,000 coat because it was cool and you thought it would impress other people, and it isn't even your style? There is a big difference there. One feels like you are a prisoner to what others think, and the other feels like freedom to live as you want.

This shift is not automatic. The old ways of thinking are

ingrained, deep, and emotionally charged. Do not under-estimate them. This shift can't just be in your brain. You have to begin to feel it in your heart.

So, what is your definition of success? What feels like free-dom to you? If it has anything to do with how much money you make or the type or quantity of stuff you have, then that is something to look at. Do you want your definition of success to be linked to your income or stuff that isn't even "you"? Is that meaningful?

I recently saw a story about a mailman who was retiring after thirty-five years. The people on his route threw a party for him. Over 300 people came to the party. According to society, this man was not a success. He was a civil servant who never made a lot of money. He was a mailman. It doesn't take a lot of skill or any education to deliver the mail. He never invented anything, cured anything, or made "an impact" on the world—probably never made over seven-teen dollars an hour. According to our societal rules, I was more successful than him when I was twenty-three years old, as I had two college degrees.

When was the last time 300 people threw a party for you to tell you they loved you? Ouch, right? How many people did this man touch over thirty-five years? How many greet-ings and smiles did he give over those thirty-five years? He was a constant in people's lives and families. All he did was deliver the mail—and he touched people every single day he did so, just by being kind and smiling. What the hell else do you want in life? That is success, people. That is "winning." That is freedom to live as you want, not as others think you should live.

I could write an entire book about people's idea of "success." Other people's idea of "success" is always going to put you into a trap, cage you, and limit your freedom. The grass is always greener on the other side of the fence. My own story is that no matter what I accomplished, I never felt successful, because I had never made a lot of money. It didn't matter what was on my résumé. I had a child at fourteen and a law degree at twenty-six. I was a good litigator and had my own law firm at age twenty-nine. I had run marathons. I had helped a lot of people and saved many children from growing up in a horrible home. None of that mattered, because I hadn't made the money I thought I should be making. I felt like a failure. It was my little secret.

I felt trapped, totally trapped. I couldn't even imagine feeling free. When I did the hard work of examining my relationship with stuff and defining what "success" meant to me, I instantly began to feel some freedom.

I had to be free. I had to do what I was meant to do with my life. I was meant to write and teach. Even if I was living in a van down by the river, but writing and teaching every day, that was what I was supposed to do. I had paid a big price to be able to write and take a break from practicing law. But I felt freedom like I had never felt before. Sometimes you have to give up everything that you used to think was important in your life to create the life that truly fits you—to be free.

Yes, we all need money in order to live. We also need money in order to ensure that we can do what we are meant to do in life. But my success and freedom didn't have anything to do with making excess money.

Maybe consider thinking about it this way. Why do you drink water? You drink water because you need it to live, you feel dehydrated when you don't drink enough, and nothing feels better than drinking water on a hot day. You drink water for the benefits it provides to your body. You don't drink it to say you drank X ounces of water that day. If you try to stockpile a bunch of water, it will get stagnant and lead to things you don't want growing in the water. Likewise, you earn money in order to provide the *water* your life needs to flourish. It shouldn't be the endgame in itself. The only purpose of money is to provide time and comfort. Any other intended purpose to acquiring or hoarding money is going to lead to continuing to try to fill the glass that has no bottom.

Additionally, if you equate success with how much money

someone has, or what they look like, or what they do, or any other external factor, you are always going to fall short. You will never be enough. You will never feel successful.

I have known people who continually compare their financial situation to others in order to measure how they are doing. Even when they think they are doing well, there will always be someone who is making more money. So, if you are making $650,000 a year and comparing yourself to people making $100,000, you feel great and successful, until you meet the couple five years younger than you who are making $5 million a year, and then suddenly, you are a complete failure. It is a no-win situation where your self-worth is dependent on other people.

When your success and self-worth are influenced by external factors, your self-esteem is at the whim of the world.

At the end of the day, who do you want to be? What life do you want to have lived?

Again, there is absolutely nothing wrong with earning a lot of money or having wealth or a luxurious lifestyle. It is about your why.

I had the privilege of meeting and spending a few days with Brian Smith, who founded the shoe company UGG. Brian certainly has made a lot of money. He lives a very nice lifestyle. His lifestyle is very him. Brian knows himself, knows his tastes, and knows what is and is not important in life. He uses his wealth for time, comfort, *and* to impact the world. He does not get his self-esteem from what he owns. That is self-evident within the first ninety seconds of meeting him. He could care less about the money other than it makes his life comfortable and allows him to impact others. Brian is the sort of person that you just want to be around. It has absolutely nothing to do with his money or what he owns. You feel like you are soaking up his kindness. That is success, people. That is success that can't be purchased.

Simplifying your life by getting rid of property that doesn't serve you can be the first step in beginning to simplify the other areas of your life. It changes the way you look at things, far exceeding your personal property.

If you only simplify your life by having only the property that serves you, that is fine, but don't be surprised if this work continues and spills over into other areas of your life and changes how you view the world. You very well may start asking yourself if other things serve you, like habits, your job, your business, other commitments, and maybe even other people in your life.

THE WORK

1.   What were you taught that "success" means?

2. After not only reading this book but also doing the work, you should have some space—literally and figuratively. Do you have the same definition of success now as you did previously?
3. If not, what is your new definition of a "successful" life?
4. Has your eighty-five-year-old self's definition of success changed at all? If so, how?
5. What does freedom look like to you?
6. How do you feel?

CONCLUSION

When you only have the possessions that serve you, fit you, and really work for you, then your problems will melt away. Um...no. Simplifying your life, only owning items that really benefit you, and, in the process, getting rid of a ton of crap, is not the magic bullet to cure all of the world's problems. What it *will* do is make navigating your life far easier. You can move more quickly, think more quickly, and have more resources to handle any issues that arise. You are just not bogged down with excess. You feel lighter and relieved. And you will feel so much better, even if you don't really think you feel bad now. You have been bogged down with so much stuff for so long that you don't even know you feel tired until you don't anymore. The relief is instant and amazing.

Someone can describe how it feels to push off the edge of a

pool and have your body glide through water, or how it feels and tastes to take that first lick of homemade ice cream on a hot summer day. However, until you actually have the experience yourself, those descriptions are complete nonsense. You just have to experience it yourself.

I can write and talk about how liberating, calming, and comforting it feels to be free of want after a lifetime of desperate searching. But until you feel it for yourself, no description can do it justice. It is the same feeling as taking off shoes that hurt your feet so badly you could cry. The feeling of a shower after an eight-hour hot hike. Crawling into your cozy bed with clean sheets at the end of a hard day. The feeling when you quietly hold a sleeping infant. It just is awesome.

When you strip away the excess, you are left with you, what you really want, and what is really important to you. What is really you?

Getting clear on your relationship with stuff is just the first step, as it is the easiest, in a lifelong journey of listening to your soul, feeding your soul, figuring out your purpose by listening to your feelings, and living as you—not living as you think you *should* be living.

Be open to where this journey may take you. Your soul is trying to speak. But it needs some quiet and for your brain to shut up. Don't worry about the whys or hows right now. If your soul is telling you to get rid of stuff, then just do it.

My journey took years, and hopefully with my sharing, your journey will be quicker and easier. Cheers to you for working to get the life that you truly want and to be free.

My life legacy in this world is to try to impact people in their daily lives—even if just a little. I want to hear your stories. I want to know how this work has impacted your life, assuming, of course, that it has. Your story will also help others who are in a similar situation and may be struggling. I would invite you to contact me with your stories at BritaLong.com.

I also want to say thank you for your time in reading my work.

ACKNOWLEDGMENTS

Writing this book has been part of my journey into a simpler and far more authentic life, and it has changed everything in my life. I don't know if I would have gotten to where I am eventually or not, but I know one thing for sure: I wouldn't have gotten here as fast as I have if it weren't for my friendship with Tucker Max. The day I met him was the day that everything began to change in my head, in my heart, and in my life. I can never adequately express my gratitude for your honesty and tough love when I needed it, your support, and your love and friendship.

To the rest of the Scribe team, your dedication to your craft and the mission of your work helped me not only write this book but create the body of work that I will do for years to come. Hal Clifford, thank you for your always-steady hand and voice, for always being honest but kind, and for having the patience of Job in editing my work. Emily, you are the calm presence in every storm. Natalie, I can't imagine writing a book without your help in keeping all of the balls in the air.

To my mentors and teachers who have taught me so much this last year about myself, moving past fear, and doing what I needed to do in order to have the life that I want, I am eternally grateful. Ilan and Guy Ferdman, thank you for not letting me give up. Philip McKernan, thank you for giving me the tools I needed to feel my feelings and heal. Kathy Dunbar, you know what you mean to me. You have saved my life more than once, and I don't know what I would do without you.

I want to thank my first simplicity clients who all signed on based on sheer faith that I could help you; I am eternally grateful.

Maria Hernandez Carter has been my avatar from the beginning, my greatest supporter, and my dear friend. You are the person who I can always turn to during the dark days and the first to celebrate with me during the bright ones.

Thank you to my friends who have always supported me and been my private cheerleaders—specifically, but not limited to, Christin and Kelly Gregerson, Christopher Miller, Sara H., Melissa Lind, Kara, Sadira, and Jayne Berg.

To my family who never question yet another "Brita" idea: I truly have the best family a person could ever want. Thank you to Jeremy and Zach, my stepsons, who I love with all of my heart and who still let me be their second mom, and to my brothers, who always have my back.

Finally, thank you to my son, Jonathan Long, who is still and will always be my everything. If I do nothing else in the world but impact you in a healthy and positive way, then I have done my bit. I want nothing more than for you to be free to live your life as you wish. I love you.

ABOUT THE AUTHOR

BRITA LONG is an attorney, writer, speaker, and life coach. Additionally, she is a mother, daughter, sister, ex-wife, business owner, and amateur trapeze artist who has wing-walked over the Salish Sea and saved two homes from certain death with full renovations.

After writing her first book in 2018 and discovering a passion for writing, speaking, and teaching, Brita decided to wind down her law practice of twenty-two years and pursue writing and teaching full time.

Brita lives in Austin, Texas with her dog, Bear. To learn more about Brita and how she can help you discover your best self, visit britalong.com.

Made in the USA
Coppell, TX
16 August 2020

33636626R00121